22 August 2020

Dear Jules,

A wonderful nostalgic one ... th
The start for a splendid 70th birthday.
I want to spend it with you ♡

V.

THE
HOLBURNE
MUSEUM

© Scala Publishers Ltd, 2011
Text © The Holburne Museum, 2011
Photography © The Holburne Museum, 2011, except
for: p. 12 (left) © John Maclean; p. 13 © Eric Parry;
and pp. 80–81 © National Theatre

First published in 2011 by
Scala Publishers Ltd
Northburgh House
10 Northburgh Street
London EC1V 0AT, UK
Telephone: +44 (0) 20 7490 9900
www.scalapublishers.com

ISBN: 978 1 85759 665 6

Text: Dr Alexander Sturgis (pp. 5–13), Matthew
Winterbottom (pp. 16–25, 40–55, 66–69) and
Amina Wright (pp. 26–39, 56–65, 70–87)
Project editors: Suzannah Angelo-Sparling
(Holburne Museum), Esme West (Scala)
Copy editor: Matthew Taylor
Printed and bound in Singapore

10 9 8 7 6 5 4 3 2 1

British Library Cataloguing in Publication Data
A catalogue record for this book is available from
the British Library

PREVIOUS PAGE:
Jacob's Ladder (detail)
English
Raised embroidery, about 1660
See p. 23

LEFT:
Garton Orme at the Spinet (detail)
Jonathan Richardson the elder (1665–1745)
Oil on canvas, about 1707
See p. 57

Preface

David Posnett, Chairman of the Trustees

The Holburne Museum was Bath's first art museum. It opened its doors to the public in 1893 and moved to its current building at the end of one of Bath's great streets in 1916. This book celebrates as significant a moment in the Museum's history: the completion of a development project that has seen the restoration of our Grade I listed building and the creation of a wonderful new extension by Eric Parry, an important and sympathetic architect of our time, who has designed the space that is needed for the Holburne to be a museum for the twenty-first century.

These new spaces will allow us to do so much more than was possible in the past. Indeed, the role of museums has changed radically since our inception: they are no longer simply receptacles for works entrusted to them. For me, perhaps the most important change is that, through our displays, our exhibitions, the work of our education team and in our role as the University of Bath's Museum, we will be able far more effectively to encourage the young to enjoy and learn from works of art, and, in doing so, to open their eyes to the great and enriching pleasure that art can afford.

The renewed Holburne not only allows us to serve our visitors much more effectively than before but also allows us to celebrate our collection, and this book is part of that celebration. Within its pages you will discover the range, variety and quality of a collection that still retains something of the character of a private collection, one assembled for pleasure and shaped by personal taste.

Our Museum was founded by an act of far-sighted generosity, and it has been enhanced and sustained by many others since its foundation and indeed continues to grow today. The restoration, if not the resurrection, of the Holburne has been achieved with the generous support of the Heritage Lottery Fund and the magnificent help of the Friends and Patrons of the Holburne and the many private donors and trusts to whom we are all indebted. In addition, we would not have in effect 'saved' the Holburne and its collection without the unstinting support of a dedicated group of Trustees, to whom I extend our sincere thanks.

We hope and believe that the Museum as it now stands meets the hopes and expectations of all those who have contributed to its future and that it will continue to inspire your support.

4

Introduction

Alexander Sturgis, Director

Like many of the best-loved museums, the Holburne has an individual's collection at its heart. The Museum continues to reflect the tastes and enthusiasms of its founder, the sympathetic if slightly shadowy figure of Sir Thomas William Holburne (known as William), who assembled his collection of everything from paintings to silver and from minerals to maiolica in the middle years of the nineteenth century. Sir William's collection has given the Museum its character and a kernel of quality and distinction, but from the start it was intended that the collection should grow, and it has. In the years since its foundation the Museum has attracted over 2,000 further gifts, bequests, loans and purchases. These have included important collections of portrait miniatures and porcelain and a charming group of seventeenth-century embroideries. But it is the collection of paintings that has seen the most significant and transforming additions, including the majority of the British eighteenth-century paintings, for which the Holburne is today perhaps most famous. In recent years spectacular acquisitions and loans of works by Gainsborough, William Hoare, Giuseppe Plura and others have given the Museum a particular strength in works with specific connections to eighteenth-century Bath. More recently still, the astonishing group of eighteenth-century theatrical paintings from the Somerset Maugham Collection, including masterpieces by Zoffany and De Wilde transferred to the Holburne from the National Theatre, have given the Museum a whole new, fitting and exciting dimension (see p. 80).

We know frustratingly little about Sir William Holburne, the fifth Baronet of Menstrie, and still less about how and why he collected what he did. He stares at us as an engagingly open-faced and curly-haired 34-year-old with the hint of a smile from the fine miniature portrait by the Bath artist Charles Jagger (**fig. 1**). But the surviving records refuse to give him a clear voice.

Few of his letters, journals or notebooks survive. Some of his acquisitions can be traced to particular sales, and the odd surviving letter shows dealers corresponding with him, but for the rest we rely on the collection itself and what we know of his family and career to arrive at a sense of the man and his motives. William was the younger son of a minor aristocratic family that settled in Bath in the early years of the nineteenth century. His most distinguished ancestor was William's grandfather Admiral Francis Holburne – the subject of a striking portrait by Reynolds – who in 1770 was briefly Rear Admiral of Great Britain. Following in his footsteps, William joined the navy in 1805 as an eleven-year-old volunteer. Within months he rather startlingly found himself at the Battle of Trafalgar, serving on HMS *Orion*. We can only assume that Sir William was proud of his participation in the country's most famous naval victory, and his Trafalgar medals are still in the collection – as is, rather more romantically, a wooden snuffbox, which claims to be made from the ladder of HMS *Victory,* down which the fatally wounded Nelson was carried (**fig. 2**).

As a younger son, William seemed destined for a naval career, but his life and fortunes changed with the death in 1814 of his beloved elder brother, Francis (or Frank). Frank had joined the army rather than the navy and fought under Wellington in the

5

1 (OPPOSITE)
Sir Thomas William Holburne of Menstrie
Charles Jagger (about 1770–1827)
Watercolour on ivory, 1827
10.2 x 7.8cm (shown enlarged)

2 (RIGHT)
Snuffbox made from HMS Victory
English
Oak, gilt metal, about 1820
3.5 x 11cm diameter

Peninsular campaign. He died when a minor wound received at the Battle of Bayonne turned septic. A desperately touching group of letters survives in the Museum – one seemingly spattered with tears – in which his slow death is played out and reported among the family. Frank left his sword to his younger brother, and it, together with a silhouette of the dashing young captain (**fig. 3**), is still in the collection.

The death of his brother, however keenly felt, changed William's circumstances for good, and for the better, putting him in line to inherit the family title and funds. On the death of his father in 1820 he immediately left the navy, and four years later, at the age of thirty-one, he set off on an eighteen-month Grand Tour of Europe, visiting Italy, the Alps and the Netherlands; this, we presume, was when some of his artistic interests were formed and his enthusiasms as a collector fired. We can only speculate as to why and how William turned to collecting. There was certainly little in his upbringing or education to suggest a connoisseur in the making. From his father he inherited a modest collection of family portraits and, presumably, some of the eighteenth-century dining silver and porcelain in the collection. His wider family may have offered role models for the young William to follow. His father's sister, the wealthy Catherine

Cussans, had a small collection of antiquities and porcelain, some of which William was to acquire after her death together with her portrait by Hoppner. Less directly, the Holburne family's connection through marriage to the Lascelles family from Harewood House, which they visited regularly, would have provided William with a spectacular model of aristocratic collecting and patronage. Closer to home but more speculatively, we can imagine that William looked on with admiration, if not awe, at the collecting appetites of William Beckford, who from 1822 was his near neighbour in Bath's Lansdown Crescent. Again William was to buy modestly from at least one of the sales that saw Beckford's collection dispersed.

Once set on the path of a collector, William bought voraciously and omnivorously, if always on a budget. He clearly delighted in the small and finely wrought, as witnessed by his collections of painted miniatures, antique and Renaissance gems and intaglios, his taste for the Rococo in silver and porcelain, his fine group of Renaissance bronzes and the many small cabinet paintings in the collection. Among the masterpieces of miniaturism he owned is a pearly Renaissance cameo (**fig. 4**), carved from agate, which shows Venus or a sea nymph emerging from beautifully cut waves, encircled by billowing drapery and perched on top of a sea monster. From over 200 years later and arguably even more astonishing as pieces of craftsmanship are two so-called 'micro-carvings' made by the German ivory carvers Stephany and Dresch (**fig. 5**). The pair worked in Bath in the 1790s, producing, for the king and queen among others, their distinctive and popular scenes in miniature, in which every blade of grass and leaf is realised.

If Sir William seems to have loved such demonstrations of the miniaturist's skill, his preference for the small may also have been prompted by his wallet and was certainly recommended by the fact that his purchases were destined for his elegant, but scarcely enormous, town house in Cavendish Crescent, which he and his ever-growing collection shared with his three unmarried sisters. An inventory made in 1874 lists the collection room by room, case by case and table by table. It is hard not to read it with a mounting sense of claustrophobia, as it reveals a house in which every room was crammed, every surface covered and every case filled with the thousands of objects that made up the collection. In his first-floor front drawing room, pictures were hung cheek by jowl against gold wallpaper, and the room was

6

3
Captain Francis Ralph Thomas Holburne
William Hamlet (active 1785–1816)
Painted on glass, about 1810
31.2 x 24.6cm

filled with twenty-one chairs, nine footstools, nine tables, five pedestals, three cabinets and a piano, most of them covered with crowded and eclectic displays of porcelain. Different areas of the collection took up residence in different parts of the house: Sir William's scholarly and antiquarian interests were reflected in the displays in the library, which included his small-scale sculpture gallery of 102 Renaissance and antique bronzes; his impressive collection of maiolica was crowded on to the first-floor landing; and his Wedgwood vases jostled for position in his second-floor bedroom.

Sir William's taste was scarcely avant-garde. In paintings the Italian and Dutch seventeenth century predominated, and the collection's great strength in Dutch genre scenes and the

4 (ABOVE)
Cameo: *The Birth of Venus*
North Italian
Agate, about 1560
3.5 x 3.5cm (shown enlarged)

7

5 (RIGHT)
Miniature ivory carving: *Garlanding the Herm*
G. Stephany and J. Dresch (active 1791–1803)
Ivory on blue glass
Diameter 6.2cm (shown enlarged)

golden-hued landscapes of the Dutch Italianate painters reflects an entirely conventional taste, famously shared by George IV. However, the individual painters best represented in the collection, in quantity at least, were local and contemporary. Nearly thirty paintings by his near neighbours Thomas and Benjamin Barker hung on Holburne's walls, including the splendid youthful self portrait of Thomas Barker and rather too many of the same artist's later muddy genre scenes and landscapes, probably bought direct from the studio.

Sir William's position as a collector and connoisseur seems to have been important to him. He acquired in the course of his life a reputation as a 'collector of distinction', lending pieces to major national loan exhibitions through the 1860s, and was elected to the Burlington Fine Arts Club in 1867. His pride in his collection and the recognition it brought him is perhaps reflected in a photograph of the 1870s (**fig. 6**), where he is shown sitting beside two of his prized porcelain figures, which we can imagine him carefully carrying to the photographer's studio as fitting props or attributes. The fact that William, and the three sisters with whom he lived, all remained unmarried and childless perhaps gave his collection even greater importance in his eyes. It certainly lay behind the decision that it should become the nucleus of a museum.

The idea that his collection should provide the beginnings of Bath's first art museum seems to have been Sir William's own,

but it fell to his younger sister Mary Anne Barbara (**fig. 7**), who outlived her brother by eight years, to make the necessary arrangements. Mary Anne Barbara appears to have been particularly exercised by her position as the last member of a disappearing family, and much of her energy and funds in her last years were directed towards perpetuating the family name. To this end she had built a new church at Menstrie, near Stirling in Scotland, where the family's name and baronetcy originated, and erected an elaborate monument to the family in Lansdown cemetery. She also insisted that the planned museum should take on the family name in perpetuity. But her anxiety to ensure the future of her brother's collection as 'the nucleus of a museum of fine Art for Bath' led to her fussing over details and drawing up an imprecise codicil to her will, which meant the early years of the Museum were ones of confusion. Legal wrangles and a protracted search for a home meant the Holburne of Menstrie Museum did not open its doors until 1893, eleven years after Mary Anne Barbara's death. It did so not in its present home but squeezed into the slightly less happy surroundings of the old Bath Savings Bank building in Charlotte Street, just off Queen Square.

In 2008 a box of glass negatives was discovered in the Museum, showing the collection installed in its first home (**fig. 8**). As at Cavendish Crescent, the paintings fill every available inch of wall space, while handsome ebonised cases, crowded with objects, stand on bare floorboards. Despite the evident constraints of space and limited opening hours, the initial signs were good. Over 5,000 visitors came in the Museum's first year, but interest was not sustained, and within a couple of years numbers had almost halved – a development the Trustees blamed on the inadequacies of the Museum building and its position.

At precisely this time, in 1897, the City received a bequest from a Mrs Roxburgh for the purpose of building an art gallery for Bath. Recognising the Holburne's unsatisfactory home, the Roxburgh Trustees wrote to the Chairman of the Holburne suggesting that 'some joint action between the Trustees of the Holburne and Mrs Roxburgh's Trustees might possibly be the best thing for the City, and there is also the possibility that if assistance could be obtained from the Corporation a very important building might be secured devoted to the purposes of the Holburne Museum and the Art Gallery'. The proposal seemed eminently sensible: Mrs Roxburgh's money was to be put towards the building of an art gallery without a collection, and the Holburne Collection wanted a proper home. Sensible it may have been, but it was dismissed immediately and out of

hand by the Holburne Trustees. Their stated reason was Mary Anne Barbara's insistence that the Museum should carry the family name in perpetuity, but it seems that political (and probably personal) animosity between the Tory Holburne Trustees and the Liberal Council played its part as well. Dr Coates, the Holburne Chairman and previously Mary Anne Barbara's physician, was particularly antagonistic towards what he saw as a threat to the Holburne's independence. His attitude may well have reflected Mary Anne Barbara's own views, and he had earlier written of her 'emphatic desire ... that no Corporation or other Society should have anything whatever to do with her bequest'. Whatever the reasons, the results were clear: the City's new Victoria Art Gallery adjoining the Guildhall opened its doors in 1900, and the Holburne Museum remained independent but aloof in its cramped home.

There was, however, a reason that the Holburne Trustees had felt able to insist on their independence. They knew that their fortunes were about to change. Sir William's wealthy aunt Catherine Cussans had established a number of trusts, which would, it was understood, revert to the Museum on the death of the last life beneficiary, a Mrs Isabel Calnady. She died in 1906,

8
Interior of the Holburne of Menstrie Museum, Charlotte Street, in 1901

and immediately the Museum's available funds were more than doubled.

But just as the Museum's financial situation was about to be transformed, it found itself facing a crisis of a rather different sort, brought on by the Museum's own recently appointed young and ambitious curator, Hugh Blaker, who was later to advise the sisters Gwendoline and Margaret Davies on their collection of pioneering Impressionist and Post-Impressionist paintings (which now belong to the National Museum Wales). Blaker, on examining the Holburne's paintings, was understandably sceptical about a number of the more wishful attributions that Sir William had given them, and, enlisting the help of Ayerst Buttery from the National Gallery, he took many of them to task. In many cases he was perfectly justified, and alas Sir William's Leonardo (**fig. 9**) and Raphael, his Titian and Holbein, his Rubens and Poussin, all withered under the two men's scholarly glare. But professional scepticism frequently gave way to aggressive suspicion, leading Blaker to dismiss almost two-thirds of the picture collection as 'bad' and to remove them from the walls. To make matters worse, seeing an opportunity to enhance his own reputation at the expense of the collection's, Blaker also went to the national press, leading the *Daily Mirror*, for example, to splash with the sensational headline '200 Spurious "Old Masters" Amazing Discovery at Bath Art Museum'.

Holburne was certainly not the only nineteenth-century collector to have accepted hopeful if not fanciful attributions for the paintings he bought, although to what extent he was deliberately misled by unscrupulous dealers is uncertain. There are certainly a few paintings in the collection that appear to have been painted to deceive – nineteenth-century paintings purporting to be by Salvator Rosa or Poussin. A tantalising but as yet unproven possibility is that some may even have been painted by Thomas Barker, through whom we know Holburne purchased some of his Old Master paintings. But if a small number of Holburne's pictures can be accurately described as fakes, recent and more temperate judgements have revealed a far more interesting and richer collection than Blaker allowed. A number of so-called 'spurious' works have been reclaimed by their artists, while many more are now ascribed to perhaps less renowned but certainly no less respectable – or indeed 'old' – masters.

9 (ABOVE)
Female Head (detail)
Mantuan School (thought by Sir William to be by Leonardo da Vinci)
Oil on canvas, about 1525
22.8 x 19.1cm

10 (LEFT)
Tankard
English (London)
Silver-gilt, 1683/84 with early 19th-century 'Elizabethan' decoration
20 x 23 x 14.8cm

INTRODUCTION

11 (LEFT)
Sydney Hotel, Bath
John Hill, after John Claude
Nattes (about 1765–1822)
Coloured aquatint, 1805
24.8 x 34.4cm

12 (RIGHT)
Sydney Gardens, Bath
John Hill, after John Claude
Nattes (about 1765–1822)
Coloured aquatint, 1805
26.1 x 34.2cm

Holburne's taste and eye seem always to have been more assured for the decorative arts than for paintings, but here too things were not always as they seemed, or as he believed them to be. An intriguing ewer, claiming to have been discovered in the excavations of Herculaneum and perhaps bought by Sir William on his youthful tour of Italy, has recently been unmasked as a nineteenth-century fake. More typical within the collection are objects that were doctored to increase their interest to the nineteenth-century collector, such as a splendid seventeenth-century tankard extravagantly disguised as a Tudor object some time in the nineteenth century, when it was elaborately embossed with Tudor roses and the figures of Elizabeth I and Lord Burghley (fig. 10).

Despite the unwelcome flurry of controversy caused by Blaker's calculated scaremongering, the Holburne Trustees, under new and energetic Chairmanship and bolstered by the arrival of Catherine Cussans's money, now turned their attention to the problem of finding a more suitable permanent home for the Museum. Even before her death Mary Anne Barbara had fastened on the empty Sydney Hotel as a fitting setting for the collection, but a sequence of legal complications had frustrated all attempts by the Museum to buy it. In 1908, with new purpose and new funds, the Holburne Trustees finally arrived at an arrangement that made the purchase possible, involving the Council buying the whole of Sydney Gardens, in which the hotel

sat, and then selling the building with a small area of garden back to the Holburne Trustees. A mere four years of legal wrangling later, the building was theirs.

The Sydney Hotel had been built at the end of the eighteenth century as a centrepiece of the planned 'Bath New Town' over Pulteney Bridge, on the estates of the Pulteney family in Bathwick. The plans for the whole development, drawn up by Thomas Baldwin, were beset with financial problems and never fully realised, but Great Pulteney Street (the backbone of the scheme) and Sydney Gardens (the pleasure gardens at its end) were both completed, as was the Hotel, which formed the fulcrum between the two. Although conceived by Baldwin, the hotel was built to a design by Charles Harcourt Masters. Two views made shortly afterwards show the two very different faces the building presented (figs 11, 12). The formal façade, with its classical portico on a rusticated base, faced down Great Pulteney Street, as it does today, creating a suitable end-point to this broad and imposing approach. But visitors passing through its arches (having paid their entrance fee) would emerge into the very different world of Sydney Gardens behind. Here they would be faced with a transparency (or translucent picture) depicting Apollo with his lyre; above their heads an orchestra would be playing, and ranged on either side were supper boxes in which to take tea, to dine and to watch the world pass by. Beyond were the many attractions of the pleasure garden itself: a labyrinth 'twice as large as Hampton Court' with an amazing mechanical swing of uncertain design at its centre, a mock ruined castle with a moat, a grotto, models of a mill, and a hermit's cottage complete with puppet hermit, as well as a network of 'serpentine walks, which at every turn meet with sweet shady bowers furnished with handsome seats, some canopied by Nature others by Art'. Here, among many others,

11

13 (ABOVE)
Sydney Hotel
Mowbray Green (1865–1945)
Photographic plate, 1911
Original plate 9 x 9cm

14 (LEFT)
Front of Holburne Museum
© John MacLean
Photograph, 2003

12 Jane Austen, who from 1804 lived over the road at 4 Sydney Place, walked and dined and attended at least two of the many evening galas in the gardens, in which music, performances, illuminations and fireworks brought further life and excitement to the surroundings.

By the time the Holburne Trustees finally bought the Sydney Hotel in 1912, the glory days of the pleasure garden were long past. In the intervening years the park had seen many changes, including, most dramatically, Brunel's Great Western Railway, cutting theatrically through the gardens in 1840 and sweeping away the labyrinth. The Hotel too changed in appearance and use: an extra storey had been added in the 1830s before, business declining, it became a school, the Bath Proprietary College, in 1853. The college left in turn in 1880, and the building had been empty since then (**fig. 13**).

In anticipation of their purchase the Trustees invited the distinguished architect and historian Reginald Blomfield, then Vice-President of the Royal Institute of British Architects, to submit proposals to transform the Hotel into a museum. Blomfield's plans went through various incarnations, his more extravagant suggestions – including a proposed grand dome – being reined in by budgets before building finally commenced in 1914. In his own words, Blomfield 'gutted' the inside of the building in order to create his two grand galleries, the top-lit picture gallery on the second floor and a spectacular high and light-filled room for the decorative arts on the first floor. Both were reached by a grand stair set on the building's axis. Blomfield was an enthusiast and scholar of French architecture, and his plan and the remodelled façade have distinct French touches, including the balustraded parapet with its flaming urns above the portico, the re-proportioned windows and the cartouches above them, which recall Ange-Jacques Gabriel's pavilions on the Place de la Concorde in Paris and the same architect's Petit Trianon at Versailles. Blomfield also removed the screen wall that originally extended on either side of the building and replaced it with an elegant colonnade, which gave on to the enclosed Museum garden behind (**fig. 14**).

But if Blomfield's interventions internally and on the façade were largely successful, they were made at a price. The placing of the stair on the central axis and the decision of the Holburne Trustees to separate the Museum from the park denied the building its original role as a gateway to the pleasure gardens and created a rear façade of cliff-like severity. Among the many things achieved by the Museum's recent extension is the welcome re-establishment of the building's original role as a gateway between the world of the city and that of the park.

The Holburne Museum finally opened its doors in its new home in 1916. A glowing review of the new displays in *The*

Burlington Magazine heaped praise on the Museum's curator, George Dudley Wallis, for his taste, judgement and arrangement and finished with the observation that 'what attracts visitors, also attracts donors'. True to this prophecy, bequests and gifts flooded into the new Museum in the years that followed, usually (but not always) building on the existing strengths of the collection. Of particular importance were gifts of Meissen and English porcelain made in the 1940s by two trustees: J. MacGregor Duncan and James Calder. In the following decades the collection of paintings was transformed through the bequests of Ernest Cook, via the National Art Collections Fund in 1955, and the former Trustee Sir Orme Sargent in 1962, which brought to the Holburne the wonderful group of portraits by Allan Ramsay and works by, among others, Stubbs, Raeburn, Turner and, of course, Gainsborough.

The steady growth of the collection was just one of the reasons, albeit one of the most important, that by the end of the twentieth century it was clear that the Holburne had outgrown its home. In the years since the building first opened its doors, the expectations and demands of visitors have also changed. Temporary exhibitions, lectures and teaching, shops and cafés have all become part of what museums provide and how museums survive, and all demand space. With these imperatives in mind and with a desire to re-establish the link between the Museum's building and the park, the Trustees launched a competition in 2002 for designs to an extension to the Museum to provide it with the space it desperately needed. From a field of over sixty, Eric Parry was selected.

Like Blomfield's before him, Parry's designs went through several incarnations: an early scheme with pavilions linked by underground passages was abandoned as too ambitious and expensive (**fig. 15**). Further changes were made as the proposals worked their protracted and at times painful way through the planning process. But throughout, Parry's scheme has sought to marry the demands of the practical requirements of the Museum with his understanding of the site and the unique position of the Museum building as the fulcrum or lens between the formal classical world of the city and the lyrical world of the one-time pleasure garden. It was this understanding that informed Parry's choice of glass and ceramic for his pavilion, which through their colour and reflectivity take on the character of their secluded and shadowed garden setting. As well as providing the Museum with the space it needs, Parry's building turns a bold and beautiful new face towards the park and re-establishes the route through the building from Great Pulteney Street to the park that was fundamental to its original purpose.

For those of us who work at the Museum and, I hope, for its visitors, however, the most exciting thing about the newly extended and refurbished Holburne is the way that the building serves the collection and allows us to show more of it than has been possible for generations in ways that make the most of its strengths and character. It is a character that still reflects the enthusiasms and enjoyment of its founding collector, an enjoyment perpetuated and enhanced by subsequent donors and successive curators. I hope it is also one that emerges strongly and enticingly from the pages of this book.

13

15
Rear Elevation at Dusk
© Eric Parry
Drawing, 2003

The Collection

Matthew Winterbottom
and Amina Wright

MAIOLICA 16

BRONZES 18

EARLY SPOONS 20

17TH-CENTURY EMBROIDERIES 22

17TH-CENTURY SILVER 24

NORTHERN EUROPEAN PAINTINGS 26

ITALIAN PAINTINGS 36

EATING AND DRINKING 40

ORIENTAL PORCELAIN 46

CONTINENTAL PORCELAIN 48

ENGLISH PORCELAIN 50

WEDGWOOD 52

THE WITCOMBE CABINET 54

BRITISH PORTRAITS 56

PORTRAIT MINIATURES 62

GEORGIAN BATH 64

THE MAUGHAM COLLECTION 80

SCENES OF GEORGIAN LIFE 82

BRITISH LANDSCAPE 86

Dish: *Diana and Actaeon*
Italian (probably Siena)
Tin-glazed earthenware
(maiolica), about 1495
Diameter 52cm

S ir William Holburne assembled one of the finest small collections of maiolica in the country. He was perhaps attracted by its vibrant colours, which, unlike many Renaissance paintings, remain as fresh and unfaded as when first made. This dish is the earliest and most important piece of maiolica in the collection. The central scene shows the tragic moment in the story, told in Ovid's *Metamorphoses*, when the goddess Diana, while bathing with her nymphs, is seen accidentally by the hunter Actaeon. In her wrath

Diana sprinkles him with water. In so doing, she transforms him into a stag, and he is hunted down and killed by his own dogs. The border of the dish depicts the violent scenes that erupted at the wedding of the Lapith King Pirithous to Hippodamia when Eurytus, fiercest of the Centaurs, attempted to carry off the bride.

The dish depicting the story known as *Shooting at Father's Corpse* is the only known example of maiolica with this subject. The story, originally taken from the Jewish Babylonian Talmud but

MAIOLICA

RIGHT
Dish
Italian (Urbino)
Tin-glazed earthenware (maiolica), dated 1526
Diameter 23.8cm

BELOW
Dish: *Shooting at Father's Corpse*
Italian (Urbino)
Tin-glazed earthenware (maiolica), about 1540
Diameter 24cm

much changed, tells of three sons who on the death of their father are told that only one of them is his real son. To determine who this is, they are told to fire arrows into his exhumed corpse. The one who turns away and cannot complete the task is revealed to be the real son. The dish is a fine example of *istoriato* maiolica – maiolica painted with a scene (usually taken from an ancient mythological, historical or biblical source) that covers the entire surface. Sixteenth-century diners would show off their Classical knowledge and erudition by indentifying and discussing the stories depicted on the dinner plates and bowls they had been eating from.

Not all maiolica was decorated with stories, however. The dish on the right is decorated with grotesques incorporating half-human monsters, trophies of arms, ribbons, foliage and vases. Grotesques became fashionable in Renaissance Italy following the discovery of such decoration on the walls of Emperor Nero's Golden House in Rome in about 1480.

MAIOLICA

St George and the Dragon
Francesco Fanelli (active 1608–1661)
Bronze, about 1635
Height 26.5cm

This figure of a kneeling woman, known as the *Crouching Venus*, is a technically superb and almost flawless bronze. It was made by Antonio Susini after a model by the famous Florentine sculptor Giambologna (1529–1608) that was itself based on ancient Greek and Roman sculptures. Antonio Susini was one of Giambologna's most important assistants in Florence until he set up his own studio around 1600. Unlike his master, Susini was a specialist bronze-caster, and the finish on the Holburne's Venus is finer than versions made by Giambologna himself.

The sculpture is prominently engraved with 'No. 35' under the left shoulder blade. This is a French royal inventory mark: the sculpture was acquired by Louis XIV in 1663 and remained in the French royal collection until the Revolution in 1789.

The wonderfully dynamic *St George and the Dragon* also has a royal connection. It was made in England by the Florentine-born sculptor Francesco Fanelli. Fanelli was summoned to England in 1635 by Charles I, who was particularly interested in his skill in making small bronzes. Fanelli received a pension from Charles I and later described himself as 'Sculptor to the King'. He made several versions of *St George and the Dragon*. A 'little S George on horseback wth a dragon by, beeing of brass upon a black ebbone wooden Peddistal' by 'the One eyed Italian ffransisco' was listed in Charles I's Cabinet Room at Whitehall Palace. The composition is derived from a painting by Raphael that had also been in the collection of Charles I and is now in the National Gallery of Art, Washington, DC.

Both sculptures were among the finest of the 102 miniature and small-scale antique, Renaissance and modern bronzes that Sir William Holburne displayed in his study.

Kneeling Woman
Antonio Susini (active 1572–1624)
Bronze, about 1600
Height 25cm

19

More silver spoons survive than any other silver objects made before 1700. Before the introduction of the fork and matching sets of cutlery in the seventeenth century, most people ate using their own personal spoon and knife. Spoons were expensive objects, costing as much as an artisan earned in a week, but they were not owned by the wealthy alone. Made and sold in almost every market town, spoons were often the only silver object (and therefore the most valuable thing) that a person owned. They were deeply personal objects: spoons were given by godparents at baptisms and exchanged at marriage and often have names and dates inscribed on them. Spoons topped with figures of the twelve Apostles were popular baptismal gifts. Each Apostle was identified with one of his attributes, often linked to their martyrdom: here St James the Greater is shown with a pilgrim's staff. Early spoons held a particular fascination for Sir William Holburne, and he amassed an impressive collection of over 120 sixteenth- and seventeenth-century examples from England, the Netherlands and Germany.

The most important spoon in the collection is this extraordinary folding combination fork, spoon and pen (right and below). It was probably made as a status object for admiration rather than for practical use. The stem and finial are decorated with miniature figures of St George and the Dragon and the kneeling princess. It was made in the workshop of Friedrich Hillebrandt, a leading Nuremberg goldsmith who supplied luxury objects to some of Europe's wealthiest patrons.

In seventeenth-century Holland spoons were sometimes given to commemorate deaths. The elaborate funeral spoon (opposite, top right) commemorates the death of Elisabeth Boser in Amsterdam in 1664, aged eleven. According to records in the Amsterdam Municipal Archives, Elisabeth was the only daughter of Jacob Boser, a shoemaker, and his wife, Annetje. This richly decorated spoon and the relatively high cost of her funeral (15 guilders) suggest that Elisabeth was greatly cherished by her family.

Folding combination fork, spoon and pen
Friedrich Hillebrandt (1555–1608), Nuremberg
Silver-gilt, about 1590
Length 18cm

EARLY SPOONS

Apostle spoon: St James the Greater
English (London)
Silver, parcel-gilt, 1534/35
Length 18.5cm

Funeral spoon for Elizabeth Boser
Dutch (Amsterdam)
Silver-gilt, 1665
Length 15cm

Seal-top spoon
Jeremy Johnson
(active 1640–1675),
London
Silver with later
gilding, 1664/67
The stem is pricked:
*John BAULDWIN was
born ye 13 of May 1667*
Length 17.8cm

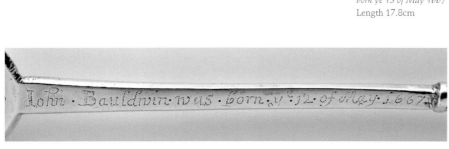

Raised embroidery: *The Restoration of Charles II*
English
Satin embroidered with silk, linen lace, metal
threads, pearl beads and mica, about 1660
31.7 x 39.6cm
Gift of Miss M A Carr, 1963

22

Most women during the seventeenth century, no matter how rich or poor, were expected to be competent at needlework. However, only a privileged few could afford the time or materials to make decorative embroidered pictures. The Holburne Museum has a remarkable collection of these: many of them, such as the two shown here, incorporate raised work (more popularly known as 'stumpwork'), the technique of embroidering over padding in high relief. Such elaborate embroideries were the culmination of years of practice by young needlewomen, designed to show off their mastery of the craft.

The Restoration of Charles II is a fine example of raised work, made by a talented needlewoman in a wealthy household during the 1660s. In the centre of the panel the young Charles II is shown hiding in the Boscobel oak following his defeat at the Battle of Worcester on 3 September 1651. Above to the right, he is seen escaping on horseback disguised as a servant with Jane Lane. In the

17TH-CENTURY EMBROIDERIES

Raised embroidery: *Jacob's Ladder*
English
Satin embroidered with silk, metal wire, glass beads
and seed pearls, about 1660
32.7 x 39.6cm
Gift of Miss M A Carr, 1961

foreground, to the left of the tree, is the mature Charles II wearing his crown and robes of state following his restoration to the throne in 1660. He is flanked by his Queen, Catherine of Braganza, and courtiers. The panel is worked on a white satin ground, embroidered in silk with linen lace, metal threads, pearl beads and mica.

The subject of *Jacob's Ladder* is taken from the Old Testament. On his journey to Haman, Jacob lay down for a rest, using stones as a pillow. He dreamed of a ladder reaching up to heaven, with angels going up and down it. From the top, God spoke to him, promising the land to Jacob's descendants, the Israelites. The composition is derived from a late sixteenth-century engraving. Among the many animals and insects that surround the central scene is a particularly charming lion with shaggy mane.

OPPOSITE
Tankard
Johann Eissler (1640–1708), Nuremberg
Silver-gilt, ivory and gems, about 1700
33 x 25 x 16cm

RIGHT
Rosewater basin
English (London)
Silver-gilt, 1616/17
Diameter 55cm

BELOW
Bell salt
English (London)
Silver-gilt, 1613/14
Height 26cm

Like many nineteenth-century collectors, Sir William Holburne was particularly attracted to richly decorated seventeenth-century silver. He assembled a small but fine collection of pieces from England, Germany and the Netherlands that he displayed on his dining-room sideboard. The German city of Nuremberg was a major silver-making centre, and its wares were exported throughout Europe. This spectacular silver-gilt and ivory tankard was made by the successful Nuremberg goldsmith Johann Eissler. The ivory is carved in high relief with the story of the abduction of the Sabine women to help populate the newly built city of Rome. The tankard is also set with colourful gems. The use of exotic and colourful natural materials such as ivory and semi-precious stones was often a feature of seventeenth-century goldsmiths' work.

Very little English silver survives from before the 1640s, because so much was melted down during the Civil War.

The magnificent rosewater basin and bell salt are therefore particularly rare. The rosewater dish, which later belonged to Queen Charlotte (1744–1818), would originally have had a matching ewer that would have held warm, scented rosewater. Wealthy and important diners would have used the ewer and basin to rinse their hands ceremonially before eating, at a time when, prior to the introduction of the fork in the 1660s, fingers were frequently used in addition to knives and spoons.

Elaborate silver salts (salt cellars) reflect the value and importance that used to be attributed to salt. The bell salt is one of only a small number of similarly shaped English salts to have survived. It can be broken down into two smaller salts and a pepper caster. The size and the position of the salt on the table indicated the status of the diner: guests were seated above or below the salt according to their importance.

The Judgement of Paris
German School
Oil on panel, between 1530 and 1550
52.3 x 39.7cm

Sir William's taste for the finely detailed extended to his collection of paintings. Although best remembered for his seventeenth-century Dutch pictures, Holburne also left a handful of earlier portraits and narrative paintings, such as this Germanic *Judgement of Paris.*

Here a well-known Greek myth is presented in medieval guise. The Trojan prince, Paris, dressed as a knight in armour, has removed his extravagantly plumed helmet and fallen asleep during a hunting expedition. In a dream he is visited by the messenger god Mercury, depicted as a robed and bearded sage. Mercury asks Paris to award a golden globe to the fairest of three naked goddesses. Each of them offers him a bribe: Juno promises riches; Minerva, goddess of wisdom, can give victory; Venus offers Helen, the most beautiful woman alive. Paris's choice of Helen was to have momentous consequences and lead to the Trojan War.

This fatal moment was a favourite subject of the German artist Lucas Cranach (1472–1553). The composition has much in common with Cranach's many versions but does not exactly resemble any of them, and is also reversed. It may therefore be based on a later print. The composition does, however, share some of its most charming details with Cranach's versions of the story, such as the knight's tiny horse and the fortification in the background, and the winning gesture of one of the female figures, awkwardly rubbing her feet together and blushing as her gaze meets ours. Curiously, this figure is winged, as though Venus has taken on the attributes of her son Cupid.

During the Renaissance, the Judgement of Paris was a popular subject in pageants and works of art associated with weddings. It represented the importance of careful choices, whether in finding a bride or, in a more abstract sense, in choosing between the active life (Juno), the contemplative (Minerva) or pleasure alone (Venus).

Robbing the Bird's Nest
Pieter Brueghel the Younger (1565–1638)
Oil on panel, date unknown
17.3 x 18cm

The Bruegel (later Brueghel) family of Antwerp produced four generations of artists. The dynasty's founder was Pieter Bruegel the Elder, whose much-loved scenes of peasant life, religious subjects and intricate landscapes were made for the bourgeois and courtly collectors of Brussels and Antwerp. His humorous depictions of country folk and their foibles carry allegorical or moralising messages, sometimes illustrating traditional proverbs. Bruegel's son Pieter Brueghel the Younger always remained in the shadow of his father; he ran a busy studio that mostly produced copies or imitations of his celebrated compositions.

This little oval painting is based on a larger, rectangular original painted by Pieter Bruegel the Elder in 1568 and now in the Kunsthistorisches Museum in Vienna. A stout peasant, a sack by his feet and a stick in his hand, points upwards to the nearest tree, where a man clings to a branch as his hat falls off. He is a thief intent on robbing a bird's nest. In the background, women go about their business among fish ponds and thatched houses, while a minute pair of white swans floats on the water. This minor incident is made telling because every detail has been depicted with such loving realism. It probably illustrates the proverb 'He who knows where the

NORTHERN EUROPEAN PAINTINGS

The Visit of the Godfather
Pieter Brueghel the Younger (1565–1638)
Oil on panel, date unknown
36.5 x 49.4cm

nest is has the knowledge. He who robs it has the nest.' It contrasts the restraint of one man, set firmly on the ground, with the precarious position of the thief.

The original on which the Holburne's version of *Visit of the Godfather* is based appears to be lost, but Pieter the Younger and his studio made many versions of it. It depicts a busy farmhouse kitchen packed with detail: a man helps a woman churn butter while a nursing mother warms herself and her baby. A little girl stretches her hands towards the fire, over which a great pot hangs, full of boiling vegetables. A couple elegantly dressed in black with fine ruff collars is welcomed into the house, followed by a plump maid. While the lady searches in her purse for coins for a little boy dressed only in his shirt, the gentleman and farmer exchange a sugar loaf. The story is a simple one: the visit of a landowner and his wife to their tenant farmers, to welcome their new baby.

In the sixteenth and early seventeenth centuries a taste for the grotesque arose in Europe, perhaps as a response to the religious and political upheavals, epidemics, inflation and seemingly endless wars of the time.

Following in the footsteps of the Bruegels, Jan van der Venne of Brussels painted low-life scenes, specialising in gypsy encampments and images of old people. Here he uses a favourite religious subject, the Temptation of St Anthony, as an excuse to invent some spectacularly hideous but also highly decorative monsters. St Anthony the Great is revered throughout Christianity as the father of the informal monastic community that grew up among hermits in the Egyptian desert in the first few centuries after Christ. His spiritual power and wisdom are well recorded, and his struggles with psychological and supernatural enemies were later expressed in legends and art.

This artist shows St Anthony kneeling at the door of his cave, attended by his faithful pig. He is tempted to the sins of the flesh by a beckoning blonde wrapped in soft satin, while Avarice rattles a bulging purse. Deeper, unnamed troubles swarm on him in the form of hallucinatory chimaeras flaunting some delightfully gruesome details: one has a skull bobbing on a snake-like neck, turkey wattles and a second head dripping from its nose. A skeletal demon with a leg-shaped excrescence growing from its face, its forked tongue described with calligraphic scrolls of red paint, crouches on the ground with its hands clasped, using mimicry to mock St Anthony.

The saint overcomes them all with the threefold weapon of prayer, fasting and scripture, indicated by his kneeling posture, the skull and the open book. The artist contrasts the swirling, shrieking movement of the gang of fiends with the peaceful rock-like silence of the hermit, who is said to have rebuffed the demons saying, 'If any of you had any authority over me, only one would have been sufficient to fight me.'

The Temptation of St Anthony
Jan van der Venne (active 1616, died before 1651)
Oil on panel, date unknown
53.1 x 73.7cm

NORTHERN EUROPEAN PAINTINGS

32

Two of the Holburne's finest portraits were produced during the Golden Age enjoyed by Amsterdam during the seventeenth century. At the heart of a worldwide trading and financial network, Amsterdam's citizens formed collections of art from all over Europe. In the middle of the century the city's artistic life was dominated by Rembrandt and his many pupils, but plenty of other painters prospered as the city and its appetite for art grew.

Rembrandt's next-door neighbour, Nicolaes Pickenoy, specialised in portraits of prominent citizens, often in husband-and-wife pairs. One of the main challenges for Amsterdam portraitists was the sober black-and-white style of dress favoured by the predominantly Protestant population, but Pickenoy makes up for the restrictions in colour by making the most of the rich variety of textures. The sitter's lustrous satin doublet is embellished with black embroidery and edged with stiff braid, while the sleeves are ornamented with rows of tiny buttons and loops. He wears a velvet cloak tied round his waist, fine lace-edged cuffs and soft leather gloves. The costume is only a support for the sitter's realistically painted head and strong, direct gaze.

Jacob Backer's lady, painted a generation later, is richly adorned with fine jewellery and is obviously wealthy, but such show would have been rare among the Amsterdam bourgeoisie of the time. The comparative sensuousness of this image, with its red velvet drapery and landscape background, reflects a change in the fashion for portraits inspired by the art of France and the southern Netherlands in which Backer specialised. The artist has enjoyed describing the details of embroidered lace, the lustre of pearls and the shimmer of the gold-embroidered stomacher, and the soft texture of wispy hair. The young lady's bloom is suggested by the roses that ramble over the balustrade and the pink evening light. The black train of her dress has been drawn up on to the table to emphasise the whiteness of the hand that rests on it.

NORTHERN EUROPEAN PAINTINGS

34

ABOVE
Landscape with a Drover
Jan Asselyn (about 1610–1652)
Oil on panel, about 1640
24.7 x 21.5cm

OPPOSITE
A Hawking Party
Philips Wouwerman (1619–1668)
Oil on canvas, about 1665
28 x 34.2cm

NORTHERN EUROPEAN PAINTINGS

One of the Holburne's greatest strengths is its collection of small 'cabinet' paintings by Netherlandish artists inspired by Italy. The so-called Dutch Italianates were originally a school of northern painters studying in Rome, impressed by its nostalgic ruins, warm light and mountainous landscapes, so different from those of the Low Countries.

Jan Asselyn arrived in Rome in about 1635. His subject was the everyday life and poetic landscape of the Roman Campagna. In this peaceful pastoral scene a drover encourages a bull, together with some sheep and a goat, around a placid expanse of water. The calmness of the lake contrasts with the drama of the glowing horizon and overhanging rocky outcrops, while the autumnal colours of the foliage add to the sense of warmth. Asselyn's golden-hued scenes are influenced by the Arcadian landscapes of the French painter Claude Lorrain (already one of the most admired

artists in Rome), but his figures are often more earthy and based on direct observation, evident here in the bony flank of the bull, seen as it catches the low light.

Roman ruins and golden southern light remained a feature of Dutch art, although the younger Italianates were less likely to experience them directly. Philips Wouwerman rarely left his native Haarlem, but Italianate elements gradually crept into his delicately painted landscapes, such as the ruined arch, statue and distant mountains in this hawking scene. Men and dogs in the shadows are brought to life with little touches of colour, and here and there the sunlight catches details such as the gate-post and the rider's game-bag. A falconer approaches through the arch with a hawk on his wrist, and an attendant in a red cap carries a saddle. The composition is dominated by the white horse, a favourite element of Wouwerman's paintings that was highly prized by collectors.

Ruins of a Temple with a Sibyl
Giovanni Paolo Panini (about 1692–1765)
Oil on canvas, about 1719
64.8 x 48.3cm

OPPOSITE
Coast Scene
Francesco Guardi (1712–1793)
Oil on canvas
48.3 x 71.1cm, date unknown
Purchased by the Holburne Society, 1933

The eighteenth century saw the rise of a new kind of imaginary Italian landscape, known as the *capriccio*. These architectural fantasies set in a picturesque landscape appealed particularly to collectors looking for Grand Tour souvenirs. Because of their decorative qualities, *capricci* were very good for furnishing rooms and were often commissioned in pairs or sets with a particular interior in mind.

Panini's *Ruins of a Temple with a Sibyl* is one of a pair of views through ruined arches. Probably early works, they owe much to the artist's training with a theatrical scene-painter. Panini was equally proficient in painting views of contemporary Rome and fantasy compositions that place famous Roman monuments and sculpture in imaginary settings. He adds life to his *capricci* with small figures that sometimes act out a story from history, myth or scripture. The woman at the centre of this composition is probably a sibyl, one of the female prophets associated with pre-Christian wisdom, and her two companions may be the apostles St Paul and St Barnabas. The real stars of the picture, however, are the overgrown urn, the obelisk carved with hieroglyphs and the massive Ionic columns that support the arch.

The ruined arch was also a favourite focal point for Francesco Guardi, a Venetian painter from the generation after Panini. Like Panini, he gained his reputation painting famous views for tourists, but as he grew older he preferred to work from his imagination, creating landscapes that combine water and sky, buildings and busy little figures in scenes with a uniquely magical atmosphere. At an imagined extremity of the lagoon where Venice joins the sea, Guardi has placed a wall so that it leads the eye through an archway to a jumble of towers and a distant view of mountains. The stillness of the scene is enlivened by everyday figures: fishermen in a boat, a woman carrying her basket of washing along the quayside, a little dog, and a crowd unloading a boat reflected in the shimmering water.

The Entombment
Giovanni Francesco Romanelli (1610–1662)
Oil on canvas, about 1638
68.6 x 53.4cm

ITALIAN PAINTINGS

As interest in art grew during the seventeenth century, new collectors emerged with smaller homes while established art buyers sought work for their private rooms. Both created a demand for smaller 'cabinet' paintings, encouraging a market in scaled-down versions of narrative scenes. During the late 1630s, when the young Giovanni Francesco Romanelli was working at the Palazzo Barberini in Rome with his master, Pietro da Cortona, he made a series of jewel-like cabinet paintings, often painted on copper. These are typified by simple classical forms and bright, pure colours, as seen in the ultramarine and ochre cloaks of the women in this *Entombment*. The dominant figure in this scene is the bloodless body of the dead Christ, as it is wrapped in a white linen sheet by the young disciples John and Mary Magdalene. Nearby, Joseph of Arimathaea prepares a stone tomb, while Jesus' mother, Mary, stands contemplating her son's body. A plump pink angel holds up the contrasting greyish arm of Jesus, pointing to the wounds in his hands made by the nails that fixed him to the cross of his execution.

For Romanelli, such a small work was unusual: he mostly painted on a large scale, producing ceiling paintings, altarpieces and tapestry designs. The later Roman painter Michele Rocca, on the other hand, made a career from his delicate, richly coloured cabinet paintings.

The legend of the Mask of Truth tells how the Roman poet Virgil (the bearded figure in the centre) invented a device to detect lies, in the form of a gaping stone mask. The suspect would place a hand in the monstrous mouth, and, if guilty of perjury, their hand would be bitten off. Here an innocent-looking young wife approaches the mask while her suspicious grey-haired husband looks on from the right, his eyes bulging. In the crowd below, a desperate young man is restrained by the authorities. He is the secret lover, who has plotted with the pretty wife to fool the oracle: pretending to be mad, he forces his way on to the steps and embraces the girl. When Virgil asks her whether she has ever been embraced by any man other than her own husband, she replies, 'None but the madman who was here just now'. The Mask of Truth accepts her statement, and she returns to her husband with her hand and her reputation intact. Virgil's lie-detector never worked again, its powers destroyed by the guile of an adulteress. Rocca's bright colours and slightly caricatured figures present this morally ambiguous story as an elegant comedy of manners.

The Mask of Truth
Michele Rocca (about 1670–about 1751)
Oil on canvas, about 1720
48.1 x 63.3cm
Gift of Professor Wickstead, 1924

ITALIAN PAINTINGS

Cup and cover
Charles Frederick Kandler (died 1778), London
Silver, 1736/37
Height 31cm

EATING AND DRINKING

The dining room was at the centre of fashionable life in the eighteenth century. The splendid cup and cover made by Charles Frederick Kandler would have been displayed on the sideboard there, with no practical function apart from showing off the family's wealth and taste. The elaborate epergne would have been placed in the centre of the table during the dessert course and dressed with fruits and sweetmeats. Eighteenth-century dining required many centrepieces, tureens, dish covers, sauceboats and condiments. Hugely expensive silver dinner services in the latest style were preferred by the wealthy. Porcelain either imported from China or made at the newly established factories at Meissen or Chelsea was often preferred for the dessert course.

Dining was very different then. For the wealthy, dinner was still the main meal of the day, but it was taken much earlier than today, usually between about two and four in the afternoon. Luncheon and afternoon tea were nineteenth-century inventions, as the dining hour steadily got later.

In the eighteenth century the fashionable English dinner was served *à la francaise*, as described in William Henderson's *Housekeeper's Instructor* of about 1790:

The first course should consist of soups, boiled poultry, fish and boiled meats, and the second of different kinds of game, high seasoned dishes, tarts, jellies etc. When a third course is brought to the table, it is to be considered rather as a dessert, it usually consisting only of fruits, and various kinds of ornamental pastry.

Diners were seated at the table already set with the dishes for the first course, arranged symmetrically in geometric patterns. Diners helped each other from the array of foods in front of them. The table would then be cleared and the dishes for the second course brought in, which would include sweet and savoury, both hot and cold. A meal was judged by the number of different dishes served during each course. Finally the table would be cleared, the cloth removed to reveal the fine mahogany dining table, and the dessert brought in.

41

Epergne, or table centrepiece
William Robertson, Edinburgh
Silver, 1791/92, with additions of 1841/42
Height 70cm

EATING AND DRINKING

Tea, coffee and hot chocolate were first introduced into Britain in the 1650s. Tea came from China, coffee from Arabia and chocolate from Central America. The concept of drinking hot non-alcoholic drinks was at first viewed with suspicion. Weak 'small' beer had been the staple drink: it was safer than water and was drunk by everyone. Although these new hot drinks were initially drunk for their stimulative qualities, they soon became highly fashionable. A plethora of new objects, made of expensive silver and porcelain, appeared with which to make and serve these drinks.

The cost of importing them from far overseas combined with high taxation made them affordable for only the very wealthy. In the mid-eighteenth century black tea cost 14 shillings a pound, the equivalent of a week's wages for a skilled craftsman. In 1784 tea duty was slashed to combat smuggling, so that by the end of the century tea was drunk by all but the poorest households.

Coffee was initially more popular than tea or chocolate. By 1675 London had over 200 coffee houses. However, by the early eighteenth century English imports of tea were massively outstripping those of coffee and chocolate. The addition of cream or milk and sugar made black tea more acceptable to British palates. Tea-drinking at home (usually after dinner) became an essential part of fashionable 'polite' life. It was the woman's responsibility to make and serve the tea and to conduct polite conversation.

The development of the English porcelain industry from the 1740s was stimulated by the rising demand for tea wares. Tea was drunk from Chinese-style tea bowls; coffee cups had handles and were narrower and taller, while cups for drinking chocolate usually had two handles and covers. Worcester porcelain was particularly suited to tea wares because it was less likely to crack when hot liquid was poured into it.

OPPOSITE ABOVE
Saucer: *Love in a Garden*
Worcester Porcelain Factory
Soft-paste porcelain, about 1770
Diameter 12.2cm
Bequest of Mrs James Calder, 1954

OPPOSITE BELOW
Tea bowl, coffee cup and
covered chocolate cup
Chelsea Porcelain Factory and
William Duesbury & Co
Soft-paste porcelain,
between 1752 and 1758 and about 1770
Chocolate cup bequest of James Calder, 1944

BELOW
Cow creamer
John Schuppe (active 1753–1777), London
Silver, 1755/56
9.8 x 4.3 x 4cm

ABOVE
Tea kettle, stand and lamp
William Shaw II and William Preist
(active 1749–1759), London
Silver, 1755/56
38 x 26 x 17cm

EATING AND DRINKING

Tankard
William Lutkin (active
1699–1749), London
Silver, 1703/04
26 x 22 x 14.5cm

Punch ladle
David Hennell I (active 1734–1773), London
Silver and fruit wood, 1741/42
Length 41.2cm

OPPOSITE
Two wine glasses and a dwarf ale glass
English
Lead glass, wine glasses about 1725–50,
ale glass dated 1813
Wine glasses purchased in 1928, ale glass bequest
of Mrs Nora Cleveland Holmden, 1982

EATING AND DRINKING

Despite the massive growth in the popularity of tea, coffee and hot chocolate in the eighteenth century, vast quantities of alcohol were still drunk. One commentator of many wrote in the 1730s: 'The English are too apt to reproach Foreigners, particularly the Germans and Dutch with the vice of Drunkenness, yet none are more guilty of it than themselves.'

Although the large silver tankard by William Lutkin is ostensibly for beer, it was probably intended for display on the sideboard rather than for practical use. Beer was still drunk, especially by the poorer and middle classes, but it was no longer the staple drink it had previously been. Beer mugs and tankards were made of all manner of materials, from expensive silver and porcelain to leather and wood. Dwarf ale glasses appeared in the late eighteenth century, for ladies to drink the new clear ales brewed in Burton upon Trent.

Glass had replaced silver as the preferred material for drinking wine during the seventeenth century, particularly following the development of lead glass by George Ravenscroft in the 1670s. Wine glasses were usually kept on a buffet or sideboard and brought to the diner by a footman when requested. They were made in a bewildering number of different types and styles. Their stems incorporated air twists, bubbles or coloured glass.

Following dessert, the men would often stay at the table to carry on drinking while the ladies retired to take tea. This English custom of segregation was often adversely commented on by foreign visitors. It was during these after-dinner drinking bouts that huge quantities of wine, spirits and liqueurs were drunk. Punch was enormously popular. Made from five key ingredients of spirits (usually rum), sugar, spice, lemons and water, the name is perhaps derived from *panch*, the Hindi word for 'five'.

Large dish
Japanese (Arita)
Porcelain, about 1700
Diameter 54cm

True porcelain was first made in China in the eighth or ninth century. It is made from a mixture of china clay (kaolin) and china stone (petuntse), fired in a kiln to a very high temperature. This fuses the materials to create a white ceramic body that is hard, non-porous, translucent and capable of being very finely potted. Although exported to the Middle East from the fourteenth century, it was not until the sixteenth century that Chinese porcelain began to reach Europe. After 1700 exports of Chinese porcelain to Europe were massive. The southern port city of Guangzhou (Canton) was the centre of this trade. At any one time twenty or thirty European ships might be anchored outside the harbour, waiting to load cargoes of tea, porcelain, lacquer and silks. One ship alone might carry as many as 250,000 pieces of porcelain.

Sir William Holburne possessed over 400 pieces of Chinese and Japanese porcelain. He preferred the colourful *famille verte*

(opposite below) and *famille rose* enamel palettes and subjects of Chinese export ceramics of the K'iang Hsi period (1662–1722) and Ch'ien Lung period (1736–1795) to earlier blue-and-white wares. He also inherited a large Chinese dinner service (opposite above) decorated with the arms of his grandfather Admiral Francis Holburne (1704–1771).

Japanese porcelain was first made in the late sixteenth century. Production was stimulated by the closure of many Chinese kilns following the collapse of the Ming dynasty. By the late seventeenth century huge quantities were being exported to Europe. Imari ware (above) was particularly popular. Although made in Arita, it was named after the port of Imari, from where it was shipped. It is characterised by densely patterned decoration of flowers and foliage in underglaze blue and iron red and is often richly gilded.

ORIENTAL PORCELAIN

Soup dish from Holburne armorial service
Chinese
Porcelain, about 1749
Diameter 23cm

Dish
Chinese
Porcelain, about 1700
Diameter 25cm

ORIENTAL PORCELAIN

Sometimes known as 'white gold', Oriental porcelain was a highly prized luxury in the West. Its fineness, colour, strength and, above all, translucency were unlike anything made in Europe, whose kings and princes were eager to establish their own porcelain factories as status symbols. However, the secrets of porcelain production were closely guarded by the Chinese. Artificial porcelain, known as 'soft-paste porcelain', was first made in Florence in the 1570s, using a large proportion of ground glass to give translucency. Augustus the Strong, Elector of Saxony, was a passionate collector of porcelain; it was for him that true (or hard-paste) porcelain, using china clay and ground alabaster, was first made in Europe at Dresden in 1708. A royal factory was established in nearby Meissen two years later. Early works at the factory were copies of Chinese and Japanese pieces (left), but by the 1720s distinctly European styles had emerged (right). The Holburne Museum has an important collection of early Meissen porcelain from the collection of A E MacGregor Duncan.

Despite Meissen's best efforts to keep it secret, the process of making true porcelain, known as the 'Arcanum', soon spread to other factories and eventually throughout Europe. In France, china clay was not discovered until much later in the century and true porcelain was not made there until the 1770s, but a superior soft-paste porcelain was developed at the Vincennes factory in the 1740s. By the time the factory moved to larger quarters in Sèvres, it had the financial support of Louis XV, who was the factory's sole owner by 1759. From the beginning the factory used leading artists to design shapes and to provide drawings and prints for the porcelain painters. Innovative new shapes, styles of decoration and superb quality – all epitomised by the delicate cup and saucer (below) painted with sepia landscapes – ensured that by the 1750s the Sèvres factory had replaced Meissen as the leading centre for European porcelain production.

CONTINENTAL PORCELAIN

Bottle vase
Meissen Porcelain Factory
Porcelain, about 1723–25
22.5 x 8 x 8cm
Bequest of A E MacGregor Duncan, 1963

OPPOSITE BELOW, LEFT AND RIGHT
Cup and saucer: *goblet litron*
Sèvres Porcelain Factory
Soft-paste porcelain, 1788
6.7 x 9 x 6.9cm

49

RIGHT
Tankard and cover
Meissen Porcelain Factory
Porcelain and silver, about 1725–30
22 x 15.5 x 11.2cm
Bequest of A E MacGregor Duncan, 1963

CONTINENTAL PORCELAIN

Plate
Chelsea Porcelain Factory
Soft-paste porcelain, between 1752 and 1758
Diameter 23.3cm

Dish
Worcester Porcelain Factory and James Giles
(1718–1780)
Soft-paste porcelain, about 1770
Diameter 22.9cm

ENGLISH PORCELAIN

The English started making porcelain rather late compared with the rest of Europe. From the early 1740s a number of factories appeared in England that made artificial or soft-paste porcelain. Until the discovery of china clay in Cornwall in the 1760s, it was not possible to make real or hard-paste porcelain in England. Several of the factories, most notably Chelsea, used a type of soft paste that incorporated a large proportion of ground glass. This porcelain had a tendency to slump or distort in the kiln as the glass melted. In contrast, the early Bristol and Worcester factories used ground soap rock or steatite. This proved to be the best of the soft-paste recipes, and Worcester produced a porcelain that did not craze and which could survive the addition of boiling water to tea pots: other factories, notably Derby, had problems with their tea pots 'flying' (i.e., breaking) on the addition of boiling water. The Bow factory added ground bone ash to its soft-paste formula. This was to prove highly significant, as it eventually led to the development of bone china in the 1780s.

Unlike most Continental factories, none of the English porcelain makers had royal or aristocratic support or protection. Most were started by middle-class merchants and craftsmen. In the southwest, Quaker merchants played a significant role in establishing factories in Bristol, Worcester and Plymouth. Despite the drawbacks of its glassy paste, Chelsea always produced the highest-quality and most expensive English porcelain. Its products were highly fashionable and aimed at wealthy and aristocratic customers. Bow and Worcester concentrated on providing useful wares – for example, tea sets – to the growing middle classes.

Early English soft-paste porcelain has a particular charm and character that has made it popular with collectors since the eighteenth century. Sir William Holburne amassed a fine collection of Chelsea pieces.

Figure: *Kitty Clive*
Bow Porcelain Factory
Soft-paste porcelain, about 1750
25.2 x 15 x 12cm
Given by the Holburne Society in memory of James Calder, 1946

51

Vase
Wedgwood Ceramic Factory
Jasperware, about 1785
22.5 x 11 x 9cm

Josiah Wedgwood (1730–1795) was the twelfth and youngest child of a family of potters in Burslem, near Stoke on Trent. From an early age he began to experiment with new materials and processes that were to lead to his extraordinary success and lasting fame. In 1768 Wedgwood went into partnership with Thomas Bentley (1730–1780), a Liverpool merchant of great education, culture and ability. Bentley introduced Wedgwood to rich, aristocratic clients, and the two established a modern, purpose-built factory, named Etruria, in honour of the potters of ancient Greece and Italy. It was located beside the new Trent and Mersey canal, which provided transport for the factory's products to seaports and to his large London and Bath showrooms. In 1769 Wedgwood announced his intention of becoming 'Vase-Maker General to the Universe'. He made thousands of vases to be sold as ornaments for fashionable neo-classical interiors.

Wedgwood developed new types of coloured stoneware bodies. These included caneware, rosso antico, white terracotta and the popular black basalt that was coloured using an effluent of the Staffordshire coalmines. In 1771 Wedgwood began a series of 5,000 experiments to achieve his most famous invention, jasperware. It was perfected by 1775. This dense white stoneware could be stained throughout with metal oxides to produce consistent blue, green, lilac or brown grounds, to which decorative low-reliefs in a contrasting colour were applied. Wedgwood employed talented artists to design sculptural decoration for his jasperware vases and useful wares. Among those who worked for the firm were the sculptors John Flaxman and John Bacon, the painter George Stubbs and a group of women, including Lady Diana Beauclerk, Emma Crewe and Lady Elizabeth Templetown. Wedgwood's jasperware is perhaps his most instantly recognisable product today. It was used to produce a huge range of objects, from large vases to tiny buttons.

WEDGWOOD

Lamp
Wedgwood Ceramic Factory
Black basalt ware, about 1780
23 x 21.5 x 10cm

53

WEDGWOOD

During the late seventeenth and early eighteenth centuries lacquer cabinets, imported from China and Japan, were highly fashionable, expensive luxuries. Although decorated with Oriental-style scenes, this cabinet-on-stand was made in London. The cabinet is decorated all over its visible surfaces with the highest-quality japanned decoration.

Japanning was developed by European craftsmen, who used a combination of paints, pigments and varnishes to imitate the smooth glossy surface of oriental lacquer. Most japanned cabinets imitated the standard form of black and gold lacquer, although blue, red and green grounds were also popular. However, this cabinet, from Witcombe Park in Gloucestershire, has multicoloured decoration against a white or ivory background that more closely resembles Chinese porcelain. The layers of varnish have since darkened, giving the cabinet a yellowish hue. It is beautifully executed, with great delicacy and vibrant colours. The interior drawers are decorated with charming vases of flowers, landscapes, figures, birds and lively insects, which gleam against the pale background. Only about a dozen pieces of ivory-ground japanned furniture of this date survive.

The Witcombe Cabinet is the largest and the finest of a group of four similarly decorated cabinets that all appear to have been made in the same unidentified London workshop. The silvered stand and cresting are also remarkable survivals. Unlike the cabinet itself, they are purely European in style. They are made of carved pine, over which a thin layer of silver leaf has been applied. This was to imitate the fabulously expensive solid silver furniture that Louis XIV had made fashionable at Versailles. The cresting on top of the cabinet has small brackets for the display of porcelain imported from China and Japan.

The Witcombe Cabinet
English
Japanned and silvered wood,
about 1697
203 x 120 x 60cm
Accepted by HM Government in lieu of
inheritance tax and allocated to
the Holburne Museum, 2005

THE WITCOMBE CABINET

Until the eighteenth century, portrait painting in England was dominated by immigrant artists from the Low Countries and Germany, following in the footsteps of Holbein and Van Dyck. Willem Wissing came to London from Holland around 1676 and was soon painting for the King and courtiers. This portrait of the Earl of Rochester, Lord High Treasurer to James II, is a superb example of his work, acquired by Sir William Holburne from Forde Abbey in Dorset, where it had probably hung for over 150 years. Recent cleaning has revealed the artist's meticulous attention to detail

OPPOSITE
Laurence Hyde, Earl of Rochester
Willem Wissing (about 1656–1687)
Oil on canvas, about 1685
123.8 x 97.8cm

RIGHT
Garton Orme at the Spinet
Jonathan Richardson the elder
(1665–1745)
Oil on canvas, about 1707
122 x 96.5cm
Bequest of Sir Orme Sargent, 1962

57

and texture in painting Rochester's shimmering robes and Order of the Garter insignia, the satin-lined velvet cloak, the handmade silver lace, the enamelled St George pendant and the fluffy ostrich feathers. This politician seems very much at ease in his heavy wig and regalia, as though wearing a sword and huge gold tassels were as natural as leaning on a pedestal.

A generation later, carrying a sword was still the mark of a gentleman, even a ten-year-old one. Garton Orme, son of a Sussex squire, has been depicted by Jonathan Richardson, one of the first

English-born painters to lead his field as a portraitist. The emphasis here is on young Master Orme's accomplishments, his musicianship and elegant deportment. The low viewpoint, combined with the boy's direct gaze, give him an air of superiority. In adult life Garton Orme failed to live up to the charm of this early portrait. He incurred considerable debts, sold half the family property and is said to have murdered his wife.

58

OPPOSITE
John Sargent the Elder
Allan Ramsay (1713–1784)
Oil on canvas, 1753
125 x 100cm
Bequest of Sir Orme Sargent, 1962

RIGHT
Rosamund Sargent, née Chambers
Allan Ramsay (1713–1784)
Oil on canvas, 1749
75.9 x 63.2cm
Bequest of Sir Orme Sargent, 1962

59

Allan Ramsay came from Edinburgh, the son of the celebrated poet of the same name. After studying in Italy he settled in London, where his polished but intimate style of portraiture, his confidence and his connections among the intelligentsia quickly won him admirers. As Principal Painter in Ordinary to George III, he and his studio created dozens of official portraits of the King and Queen.

In 1749 Ramsay made a pair of portraits to celebrate the marriage of his friends John Sargent and Rosamund Chambers. Sargent was a successful businessman who did much to promote overseas trade. Commenting on their happy marriage, Ramsay described him as 'one of the most domesticated men you ever saw'. This portrait of Rosamund is unusual for the bold directness of her gaze, framed by her white bobbin-lace cap and strongly lit from the left, suggesting intimacy and informality and recalling Horace Walpole's words: Ramsay 'was formed to paint women'. The contrast between the accomplished handling of the cap and the more crudely painted black lace mantle suggests that some details of the dress may have been finished by a drapery painter.

Four years later Rosamund's father-in-law also sat to Ramsay. John Sargent the Elder was a grocer from Plymouth who became a naval accountant, and Ramsay has depicted him as a middle-class businessman in a sober grey coat. Unlike most of his contemporaries when sitting for a portrait, Sargent wears no lace, metal buttons, embroidery or luxurious dyed silks. Only the polished surface of the table and sheen of the crimson upholstered chair add richness to the composition, without detracting from the powerful characterisation of this shrewd and confident sitter.

BRITISH PORTRAITS

BRITISH PORTRAITS

The eighteenth century saw the rise of a new type of portrait known as the the 'conversation piece'. Mostly small in scale, these informal group portraits depicted a family or a gathering of friends in a stylised representation of their home or an idealised landscape.

One of the best-known painters of conversation pieces is Arthur Devis, whose portraits of country gentry are a fascinating record of Georgian domestic life, fashion and manners. This image of the middle-aged Clarke sisters of Walford Court, Ross-on-Wye, is particularly unusual in depicting women as landowners. They inherited their estate from the celebrated bachelor philanthropist John Kyrle, a distant cousin and close neighbour. The landscape probably shows the grounds of Hill Court, where the sisters lived, with Walford church and the River Wye in the background. The blue gown worn by the sister on the left was almost certainly painted from a studio prop, as it is identical to one found in two other works by Devis. The artist owned a stock of miniature costumes to be worn by jointed wooden mannequins that he used to work out the poses and gestures of his subjects.

Although George Stubbs began as a portrait painter, he soon became famous for his extraordinary portrayals of horses. This group of gentry with their horses was commissioned to celebrate a change of fortune: the Revd Robert Carter lived for many years as a quiet country parson until, in middle age, he married a young heiress and unexpectedly inherited two large estates. He later changed his name to Carter Thelwall. Carter, his wife and daughter are pictured on a drive through their estate in Lincolnshire where an avenue of trees leads from their house, Redbourne Hall, to St Andrew's Church, where Carter was vicar. Stubbs has placed the family to one side so that the eye is drawn to the church at the centre of the composition, whose spire points heavenwards to the source of the family's happiness.

Unknown Lady
Circle of John Hoskins (about 1585–1665)
Watercolour on vellum, about 1645
4.8 x 3.8cm

Unknown Man
Abraham Daniel (died 1806)
Watercolour on ivory, about 1795
6.7 x 5.3cm

Unknown Officer of the Royal Welch Fusiliers
John Bogle (1746–1803)
Watercolour on ivory, 1790
5.2 x 4.1cm

Unknown Man
Sampson Towgood Roch (1759–1847)
Watercolour on ivory, 1805
7 x 5.7cm
Gift of Captain F H Huth, 1916

Mrs Martha Udney
Charlotte Jones (1768–1847)
Watercolour on ivory, about 1802
7.2 x 5.9cm

PORTRAIT MINIATURES

On a sliver of ivory three inches long an artist has placed thousands of tiny strokes of watercolour to create a likeness of a princess. The young Princess Charlotte, only daughter of the Prince Regent, is depicted wearing an ermine-trimmed gown. Hanging from a chain around her neck is an almost microscopic portrait of a handsome young man, recognisable as Prince Leopold of Saxe-Coburg. Charlotte and Leopold were very happily married for eighteen months until her death in childbirth. By capturing the Princess's image on this tiny piece of ivory the artist has allowed her memory to live on in a likeness small enough to be carried in a pocket or worn as a jewel, just as she wears her husband's image over her heart.

The art of miniature uses natural pigments bound in water and egg yolk or gum to paint tiny pictures on ivory, vellum or card. Miniatures can also be made using the jeweller's craft of enamelling. The technique of painting portrait miniatures on vellum was perfected in Elizabethan England and flourished at the courts of Charles I and Charles II, when large studios such as that of John Hoskins produced portraits from life and miniature copies of full-size oil paintings.

By the eighteenth century most miniatures were painted on little discs of ivory, roughened to make the paint adhere to its surface. Most of the Holburne's miniatures use this technique, one major exception being Sir William's fine group of likenesses by Thomas Forster drawn in plumbago (pencil graphite) on vellum. His portrait of the formidable-looking Lady Clarke (p. 88) in her fashionable lace head-dress, black satin hood and fur mantle show the artist's skill with texture and detail.

Painting 'in little' was regarded as greatly inferior to work on canvas. Miniaturists were often peripatetic: many of those working in England were Irish (such as Sampson Roch) or French (such as Rochard), although very talented artists such as Abraham Daniel of Bath were able to settle in one city. Miniature painting was also more open to female artists, especially those who could supplement their income by teaching young ladies. Charlotte Jones, who later worked in Bath, taught Princess Charlotte.

Unlike life-size portraits, miniatures are peculiarly intimate and demand close examination. They were made to be treasured, but many come into museum collections long after the names of their subjects have been forgotten.

63

PORTRAIT MINIATURES

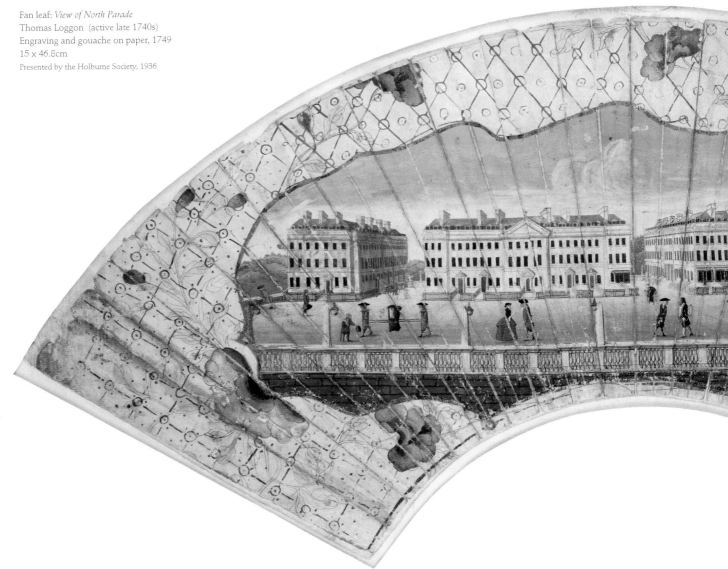

Fan leaf: *View of North Parade*
Thomas Loggon (active late 1740s)
Engraving and gouache on paper, 1749
15 x 46.8cm
Presented by the Holburne Society, 1936

64

I n a square bordered by cream-coloured stone terraces on one
side and a graceful balustrade on the other, elegant figures gather
to promenade against a sylvan backdrop of green hills. Sedan chairs
are parked in the foreground, their blue-coated chairmen leaning
over the balustrade to watch the river. They are waiting for the
Lower Assembly Rooms, with the round windows, to provide
another passenger. In the centre of the scene a gentleman greets
another, who has doffed his distinctive white hat.

This fan, with its pretty chinoiserie border, is typical of the
souvenirs to be had in Bath. Thomas Loggon specialised in fans
with topographical views and later opened a ladies' tea house and
reading room. To any of the thousands who visited Bath in the

mid-eighteenth century Loggon's view would have been instantly
recognisable as the North Parade, and the white-hatted gentleman
as the indefatigable Master of Ceremonies, Richard 'Beau' Nash.
Nash was one of the most important figures in the transformation of
Bath into England's most popular spa. The Irish artist Nathaniel
Hone's portrait of the elderly Beau is one of his most technically
accomplished miniatures and captures so much of Nash's character
and famously flamboyant clothes.

Bath had been growing steadily since the late seventeenth
century into one of the most important artistic centres in England,
second only to London. Its wealthy, discerning and leisured visitors
attracted enterprising artists to Bath from all over Britain and

ABOVE
Richard 'Beau' Nash
Nathaniel Hone (1718–1784)
Enamel on copper, 1750
5.2 x 4.3cm
Purchased 1930

65

BELOW
A Lady Taking Tea
Charles Christian Rosenberg
(1745–1844)
Painted on glass, after 1795
14 x 16.6cm

beyond: between 1700 and 1800 over 150 artists are known to have practised in Bath. Topographical artists made a brisk living selling views of the expanding city, its squares, terraces and crescents. Portraits, pictures and sculpture were available to suit every purse, as well as lessons in drawing and painting for the young people who came to Bath to improve their accomplishments.

Charles Rosenberg's profiles painted on glass are typical of the cheapest form of portrait. Like so many of his colleagues, Rosenberg arrived in Bath from abroad, probably Austria; unlike many, he was successful enough to settle in the city.

GEORGIAN BATH

Egg-shaped box in shagreen case
Probably English
Agate and enamelled gold, about 1760
5.5 x 7 x 4cm

Scent bottle
Charles Gouyn (died 1785)
Soft-paste porcelain,
between 1749 and 1759
7.4 x 5 x 4cm

During the eighteenth and early nineteenth centuries Bath was famed for its fine shops and markets. One woman who visited the city in 1788 recalled 'the beauty of the shops, which I was never tired of looking at! I could not conceive how it was possible to invent all the wants, which here were professed to be supplied'. Luxury shops first appeared in the early eighteenth century, when, following Queen Anne's visits, wealthy and fashionable visitors began to come to the city in ever-increasing numbers. Shopping became an integral part of the visit to Bath. Visitors were tempted by the latest fine silks, lace, silver, jewels, porcelain, perfumes, confectionery and countless other luxuries, such as the patchboxes printed with views of Bath and the agate egg shown here.

GEORGIAN BATH

Group of 'Bath' patchboxes
English (Bilston)
Enamelled copper, about 1790–1810
Shown approximately actual size
Gift of Mr A M McGreevy, 1998

Only the shops in London offered more choice. An early nineteenth-century visitor wrote of the 'multitude of splendid shops, full of all that wealth and luxury can desire, arranged with all the arts of seduction'.

Bath's toyshops were particularly admired. Sir Walter Scott had vivid childhood memories of 'the splendours of a toyshop somewhere near the Orange Grove'. These were not toys as we would understand them today: toys were expensive novelties intended for adults rather than children. Samuel Johnson's *Dictionary* defined a toyshop as 'A Shop where playthings and little nice manufactures are sold'. Popular toys included shoe buckles, canes, scent bottles, needle-cases and snuffboxes. Toyshops might also sell other luxuries, such as fans, porcelain, cosmetics, perfumes, hair powder and even scientific instruments. Like their customers, Bath's toyshops were supremely fashion-conscious, and news of the latest fads rapidly passed from London and Paris.

As Scott recalled, most of the toyshops were in and around Orange Grove. Between the Abbey and the Lower Assembly Rooms, the Grove was in the heart of fashionable Bath. It was described as 'spacious and well shaded, planted round with shops filled with every thing that contributed to Pleasure; and at the end, a noble Room for Gaming'.

This sculptural group is a masterpiece of charm and virtuosity. It shows the goddess Diana embracing the sleeping figure of Endymion. In Classical mythology Jupiter sent the shepherd Endymion into eternal sleep in return for the gift of perpetual youth and beauty. Each night the moon goddess Diana visited him as he lay on Mount Latmos, guarded by his dog.

The group was carved by Giuseppe (Joseph) Plura, a sculptor from Turin who arrived in Bath around 1749. In 1753 he set up his own studio in the city. *Diana and Endymion* is signed and dated 1752 and was clearly executed as a 'showpiece' for display in Plura's studio. It was admired by the connoisseur John Ivory Talbot of Lacock Abbey, who wrote to his friend Sanderson Miller on 13 August 1754: 'When at Bath, fail not to see a piece of sculpture of Endymion on Mount Patmos [*sic*], the performance of Mr Plura a Statuary.' Plura was clearly demonstrating his mastery of marble-carving for prospective clients. The group admirably shows his skills at representing a wide range of different materials and textures, from the human body to animal fur, rockwork and clouds.

The composition is clearly derived from the Pietà, the depiction of the body of Christ in the lap of Mary after the Crucifixion. Plura took the sculpture with him when he moved to London in 1755. The *Bath Journal* reported on 24 November 1755:

> At Mr Plura's, a statuary, late of the City of Bath, but now of Oxford Row, near Poland Street, London, are taken subscriptions, at a Guinea each, for a Marble Group representing DIANA AND ENDYMION: but as Mr Plura is called at an Italian Court, therefore if the subscriptions are not filled by March next, the money shall be returned to the subscribers.

However, in March 1756, on the eve of his return to Italy, Plura died of a fever.

68   *Diana and Endymion*
Giuseppe Plura (died 1756)
Marble, dated 1752
52 x 54 x 54cm
Purchased with grants from
the Heritage Lottery Fund,
the National Art Collections Fund,
the Friends of the Holburne
Museum, charitable trusts
and private individuals

Georgian Bath's longest-established artist was William Hoare. Born in Suffolk, he arrived in Bath in the late 1730s, after nine years' study in Rome. He had many influential patrons among the political and literary élite that dominated Bath culture. With his brother, the sculptor Prince Hoare, William found a niche in the burgeoning Bath market for luxury goods, as a supplier of portraits to the spa's fashionable and discerning visitors. Hoare and his studio so dominated Bath's market for oil paintings that he continued to prosper even after the arrival of the younger Thomas Gainsborough in the late 1750s.

Lettice Mary Banks is typical of the head-and-shoulders portraits that were Hoare's stock-in-trade. The daughter of an ailing landowner and MP, Miss Banks was a frequent visitor to Bath's healing waters. On her father's death she helped look after her six younger siblings and their children, including the future botanist Sir Joseph Banks. Hoare has enhanced her image with lovingly rendered lace, satin and pearls.

A decade later, the well-connected Hoare had joined a group campaigning for regular public exhibitions for artists in London. The Society of Artists held its first exhibition in 1761, and Hoare chose this family portrait of the Pitt family as his contribution. John Pitt, of Encombe House in Dorset, is depicted in a garden with his wife, Marcia, and their first child, William Morton Pitt. William is still wearing an infant's frock, while his mother wears a very soft, informal gown. Stylistically, the portrait shows that Hoare was a follower of fashion rather than an innovator: the bright, fresh colours indicate the influence of Van Dyck, and the graceful arrangement of the figures, the husband and wife placing their hands together like a couple of dancers, is borrowed from Van Dyck's famous 1635 portrait of the Herbert family, which Hoare may well have seen at Wilton House.

ABOVE
Lettice Mary Banks
William Hoare (about 1707–1792)
Oil on canvas, about 1746
57.5 x 43.8cm
Purchased with grants from the MLA/V&A Purchase Grant Fund, the Art Fund and a Patron of the Museum, 2003

OPPOSITE
The Pitt Family of Encombe
William Hoare (about 1707–1792)
Oil on canvas, between 1758 and 1761
118 x 140cm
Purchased with assistance from the MLA/V&A Purchase Grant Fund, the Art Fund, the Beecroft Bequest, the Friends of the Holburne Museum, a private donor and David Posnett in memory of Harold Leger, 2009

The Byam Family
Thomas Gainsborough (1727–1788)
Oil on canvas, 1762–66
238.5 x 229.7cm
On long-term loan from the Andrew Brownsword
Arts Foundation

GEORGIAN BATH

Thomas Gainsborough first came to Bath in the winter of 1758/59. The sixteen years he spent in the city transformed his career as a painter. He arrived from his native Suffolk as a minor provincial portrait artist and left ready to take on the most fashionable painters in London. Bath offered not only opportunities to paint the great, the rich and the beautiful but also the inspiration of the picturesque landscape that surrounds the city. From 1760 Gainsborough and his family occupied a large, newly built house, the most expensive in Bath, next to the Abbey. In 1766 they moved to a new house in the Circus, where they remained until returning to London in the autumn of 1774.

When George Byam and Louisa Bathurst first visited Gainsborough's Bath studio, probably very early in the 1760s, they were recently married. The artist depicted the plantation owner from Antigua and his aristocratic wife wandering alone in a landscape. However, contemporary accounts note that the painting was still in Gainsborough's studio in 1766, and X-ray analysis has shown that the Byams' daughter Selina was added to an apparently finished composition, painted on top of her mother's skirts. At the same time Gainsborough altered Louisa Byam's hair-style and repainted her gown to change the colour from pink to blue, using some of the original warm pink paint of the gown as a ground for Selina's face. These extravagant alterations to an already lavish canvas were made in the name of fashion, although it was not uncommon for a first child to be added to an engagement or marriage portrait a few years later. By including the shyly smiling little girl alongside her parents, Gainsborough has added a note of lightness and humanity to this swagger portrait. As Selina peeps out playfully from under her mother's lace mantle, she catches the viewer's eye and welcomes us into her parents' very private paradise.

Robert Craggs Nugent, later Earl Nugent
Thomas Gainsborough (1727–1788)
Oil on canvas, about 1761
235 x 150cm
On long-term loan from a private collection

Louisa Skrine, Lady Clarges
Thomas Gainsborough (1727–1788)
Oil on canvas, 1778
126 x 100.5cm
On long-term loan from the Victoria Art Gallery, Bath &
North East Somerset Council

Like Hoare, Gainsborough was interested in the opportunities offered by exhibiting his work in London, and he was a founder member of the Royal Academy in 1768. His first contribution to a public exhibition was this full-length portrait of the Bristol MP Robert Craggs Nugent, shown (like Hoare's portrait of the Pitt family, p. 71) at the Society of Artists' exhibition in 1761.

A contemporary described Nugent as 'a jovial and voluptuous Irishman'. He worked his way up the ranks from a remote Irish estate by marrying a succession of rich widows and gained a reputation in Parliament for his witty speeches. In 1776 his political efforts were rewarded when he became Earl Nugent. Gainsborough has captured Nugent's relaxed good humour as he sits with one leg casually crossed over his knee, catching the viewer's eye. His dark, sober suit is enlivened with glimpses of a bright red waistcoat.

By the time he returned to London after sixteen years in Bath, Gainsborough's style had changed as his brushwork became looser and more expressive and his portraits less formal. This change is evident in the artist's treatment of the satin gown and powdered hair of Lady Clarges and the blurring of her fingers as they fly over the strings of her harp.

The eighteen-year-old Louisa Skrine's portrait was painted for Sir Thomas Clarges in 1778, the year after their marriage. Fanny Burney described her as 'sportive, heedless, happy, and when she chose it, captivating'. Brought up at Warleigh Manor, near Bath, she was an important patron of musicians as well as an accomplished singer and harpist.

Abel Rous Dottin
Thomas Lawrence (1769–1830)
Pencil on paper, 1783/84
35.7 x 31.2cm
Purchased with grants from the MLA/V&A Purchase Grant
Fund, the Art Fund, the Friends of the Holburne Museum
and a private donor, 2008

Samuel Dottin
Thomas Lawrence (1769–1830)
Pencil on paper, 1783/84
35.7 x 31.2cm
Purchased with grants from the MLA/V&A Purchase Grant
Fund, the Art Fund, the Friends of the Holburne Museum
and a private donor, 2008

British portrait painting in the generation after Gainsborough was dominated by Sir Thomas Lawrence, who began his career as a child drawing Bath's fashionable visitors. Lawrence arrived in Bath in 1780, after his father was declared bankrupt. From the family home at 2 Alfred Street he earned a comfortable income by making three or four portraits a week. Contemporary accounts (often advertising 'puffs' placed in newspapers by his father) marvel at Lawrence's precocity as a self-taught artist and the ease with which he could both capture and flatter a likeness.

During his seven years in Bath, Lawrence worked almost exclusively in pastel, a technique he probably learned from William Hoare. Graphite pencil drawings from this period are much rarer, and these two were probably made when Lawrence was about fourteen, like the boys they depict. The Dottin brothers were said to be friends from the artist's school days in Bristol. They are dressed in typical schoolboy outfits of the time, with long, flowing hair, high, starched collars and extravagant waistcoats.

Another parent–child enterprise centred on Bath is remembered in this portrait of Henrietta Laura Pulteney (1766–1808), who inherited vast estates from her mother in 1782 and assisted her father, William Johnstone, in their management. Together they created the elegant new town at Bathwick, extending from Pulteney Bridge through Laura Place to Sydney Gardens, where the Holburne Museum now stands. Known as 'the richest spinster in Europe', Laura became a very able businesswoman.

The Swiss-born artist Angelica Kauffmann has used a delicate small-scale format for a full-length portrait of the eleven-year-old Laura, depicted dancing through a wood and plucking flowers. Her white muslin frock, white cap and simply fringed hair look at first glance identical to those worn by her middle-class contemporaries, but the artist's almost miniaturist eye for detail reveals the quiet luxury of the heiress's outfit: the overdress is a fragile embroidered gauze, the sash has a long silk fringe and the cap is an extravagant confection of lace, frills and feathers.

OPPOSITE
Henrietta Laura Pulteney
Angelica Kauffmann (1741–1807)
Oil on canvas, about 1777
74.3 x 61.8cm
Purchased with grants from the MGC/V&A Purchase Grant
Fund, the Heritage Lottery Fund and the Art Fund, 1996

GEORGIAN BATH

LEFT
Self Portrait
Thomas Barker (1769–1847)
Oil on canvas, about 1794
78.7 x 64.6cm

OPPOSITE
Priscilla Jones
Thomas Barker (1769–1847)
Oil on canvas, about 1802
76.2 x 63.5cm
Presented by the National Art Collections Fund, 1939

The Barker family settled in Bath in 1783 with their father, Benjamin, a failed solicitor who had worked as a painter in Pontypool. His son Thomas soon showed a precocious artistic talent, nurtured by the coach-builder Charles Spackman, who in the early 1790s sent him to study in Italy.

Thomas probably made this self portrait shortly after his return from Italy. The confident young artist's portrait is full of allusions to the past: on his easel is a view of the Temple of Vesta above the waterfall at Tivoli, a reference to his recent travels around Rome. The pose, with one hand on the hip, fashionably long hair and rich ochre coat, is borrowed from the seventeenth-century master Van Dyck.

Barker returned to Bath after a spell in London in 1798 and five years later was engaged to Priscilla Jones. Priscilla's aunt offered the couple a site on Sion Hill, to the north of Bath, on which to build a home, and the architect Joseph Michael Gandy (a pupil of Sir John Soane) designed a villa for them. Named Doric House because of its severe Greek Revival style, it provided Barker with a studio and a magnificent public gallery. The artist has used a similarly Grecian severity in this portrait of Priscilla in a child-like white muslin gown, her long dark hair flowing from under a simple straw bonnet. The composition, with its two Doric columns, is borrowed from a portrait by the Renaissance master Raphael.

Four of the couple's eight children became successful artists in their own right, and 'the Barkers of Bath' dominated the city's artistic life throughout the nineteenth century. Thomas himself failed to fulfil early promise: the family struggled financially, and Priscilla was in poor health for many years before dying in a mortgaged Doric House in 1843.

GEORGIAN BATH

The Venetian lagoon shimmers in the moonlight, and a smoky lamp casts sinister shadows around a lady desperately restraining a bright-eyed man as he raises a dagger to kill her. The scene is from Thomas Otway's tragedy *Venice Preserv'd* (1682) in a revival at Drury Lane in 1762, in which the tragic hero was played by the theatre's manager, David Garrick, and his faithful wife by Susannah Cibber, one of the most able singers and actresses of her time.

As well as being a brilliant actor, Garrick was a very clever self-publicist. He worked closely with artists to enhance his image both as actor and gentleman. In turn, the artists were inspired by his extraordinary stage presence and expressive features, and attracted notice by association with his celebrity. None owed more to Garrick than the German painter Johan Zoffany, who made his name as a portrait painter with a remarkable series of theatre scenes, in which Garrick appears in a variety of characters. He made four versions of *Venice Preserv'd* , and it circulated widely as an engraving.

This is one of a handful of works by Zoffany owned by the novelist and playwright William Somerset Maugham, who gave his collection of over eighty Georgian theatrical paintings to the National Theatre in 1951. In 2010 they were transferred to the Holburne Museum and the Theatre Royal, Bath.

Samuel De Wilde specialised in full-length portraits of actors in role; Maugham speaks of them as the pin-ups of their day. From his studio in Covent Garden, De Wilde kept up a constant production line as actors came to pose for him in costume. This portrait from Sheridan's revival of the *Merry Wives of Windsor* in 1802 is unusual for its outdoor scenery, representing Windsor Forest. The comic actor Thomas Collins trained as a musician in Bath but followed his father into the theatre.

OPPOSITE
David Garrick as Jaffier and Susannah Cibber as Belvidera in "Venice Preserv'd"
Johan Zoffany (1733–1810)
Oil on canvas, about 1764
101.5 x 127cm
The Somerset Maugham Collection

ABOVE
Thomas Collins as Slender in 'The Merry Wives of Windsor'
Samuel De Wilde (1748–1832)
Oil on canvas, 1802/03
73.5 x 57cm
The Somerset Maugham Collection

THE MAUGHAM COLLECTION

The Georgian art market supported many types of painting. Among the newest were so-called 'fancy pictures' – portrayals of unnamed, often imagined, country folk or the urban poor. They combined the realism of Dutch Golden Age character heads with the sentimentality of the French Rococo style, often with the growing market for decorative prints in mind.

Henry Robert Morland exploited their commercial possibilities particularly well. His French-inspired 'fancies' of captivating servant girls were made into fine mezzotint engravings by his pupil Philip Dawe, and he often produced several versions of the same work. The Holburne's *Lady's Maid* is one of five versions, all exhibited over a twelve-year period and sold to aristocratic patrons. While Morland's vision of domestic service reminds us that at one time all linen had to be washed by hand, this pretty maid, with her slender white fingers, neat cap and figured silk gown, is very far from the realities of eighteenth-century laundry work.

A generation later, the ardently Christian John Russell had no illusions about poverty, although his work was tempered by a melancholy sentimentality that ensured its commercial success. Like Morland, Russell made many fancy pictures for the print market, specialising in children at play. A prolific and outstanding portraitist, Russell excelled in pastel, a technique he described in his manual *Elements of Painting with Crayons* (1772). The soft texture and bright colours of the medium were ideal for images of children, such as this little match boy with his vivid cheeks, ragged coat and fluffy dog. The boy is selling two staples of the poorest street traders: crudely printed ballad sheets (the 'Love Songs' of the title) and bundles of home-made matches. His large, bright eyes, gazing straight at the viewer, are echoed by the dog's as it begs on its hind legs. One of Russell's finest works, this was exhibited at the Royal Academy in 1793.

ABOVE
Love Songs and Matches
John Russell (1745–1806)
Pastel, 1793
91.5 x 71cm
Bequest of Ernest E Cook through the National Art
Collections Fund, 1955

OPPOSITE
A Lady's Maid Soaping Linen
Henry Robert Morland (about 1716–1797)
Oil on canvas, between 1765 and 1782
70.5 x 62.3cm
Gift of Mrs Inez Murray, 1978

The rise of middle-class sensibility in Britain generated a taste for art and literature that demonstrated an awareness of society and the misfortunes of others. Following the lead of William Hogarth, artists turned from traditional history subjects to examine the lives of their contemporaries.

During the latter part of his career Joseph Wright chose affecting subjects drawn from contemporary literature, often with the advice of the poet William Hayley. *The Dead Soldier* was one of the most successful of these, and Wright and his followers made several versions. The Holburne's may be a replica. The subject is taken from a passage in *The Country Justice,* by the Somerset poet John Langhorne, that exhorts kindness to vagrants born in unfortunate circumstances, such as the child of the soldier killed fighting for his country. In Wright's view, the baby's mother crouches in a makeshift tent mourning over her soldier while the battle continues, glimpsed through foliage. The baby's pink hand clutches the corpse's white one, while his eyes gaze out pitifully at the viewer. With inadequate provision for soldiers' widows, he will have to make his own way in the world.

The subject of justice for soldiers' families is also found in George Morland's *The Deserter Pardon'd,* the last in a series of four scenes that tell how a simple country lad enlists as a soldier only to run away home to his wife. In this happy ending the deserter is pardoned and restored to his family. As she kneels in gratitude, the pretty wife grasps the generous captain's hand. The deserter, in civilian clothes, averts his eyes to see his little child joyfully clutching his leg. Like his father, Henry Robert Morland, George Morland operated at the more commercial end of the art market. Much of his painting was done for the publishers of decorative prints, and he specialised in sentimental or rustic subjects that sold well.

OPPOSITE
The Dead Soldier
Attributed to Joseph Wright of Derby (1734–1797)
Oil on canvas, about 1789
60.9 x 73.7cm
Presented in memory of Dr J Maurice Harper, 1939

ABOVE
The Deserter Pardon'd
George Morland (1763–1804)
Oil on canvas, 1792
54.4 x 45cm
Bequest of Ernest E Cook through the National Art Collections
Fund, 1955

SCENES OF GEORGIAN LIFE

Flatford Mill from the Bridge
John Constable (1776–1837)
Oil on canvas, between 1814 and 1817
24.1 x 19cm
On long-term loan from a private collection

Pembroke Castle
Joseph Mallord William Turner (1775–1851)
Watercolour on paper, about 1829/30
29.8 x 42.6cm
Bequest of Ernest E Cook through the National Art
Collections Fund, 1955

BRITISH LANDSCAPE

Just as British artists turned from history to contemporary life for narrative subjects, so they looked to their native countryside and the everyday realities around them for inspiration. Early in the nineteenth century they began to take their palettes outdoors to capture nature directly in paint, rather than working from sketches in the studio. Turner and Constable were almost exact contemporaries. As a prolific and unique topographer, Turner toured widely in Britain and the Continent, whereas Constable drew almost exclusively on his native Suffolk and the south of England.

This energetic little open-air sketch depicts one of Constable's favourite subjects, his father's mill on the Stour at Flatford, in the distance on the left. An angler sits on the bank in the shade of sunlit trees. Constable's childhood memories of the Stour developed into a nostalgia that became a driving force in his art. He spent years filling sketchbooks and boards with material from Flatford that he called upon later for the great 'six-footers' exhibited at the Royal

Academy. The first of these, *Scene on a Navigable River* (1813), is a view of Flatford very close to this study. Constable's rapid outdoor sketching captured a momentary effect and the constantly changing weather. The density of undergrowth is echoed by his use of heavy, thick paintwork.

Turner's watercolour of Pembroke Castle grew not so much from personal sensibility as from a commercial transaction: it was one of ninety-six watercolours made to illustrate the engraver Charles Heath's publication *Picturesque Views in England and Wales*. The artist gathered material from recent tours and drew on forty years' travel around Britain to cover many different aspects of contemporary life. In his image of an ancient castle Turner suggests how present-day activities are carried out against the background of the past. The fishermen on the shore load a basket with their assorted catch, while boats still at sea are tossed about by a recent squall, and the sun breaks through the clouds.

Index

Dorothy,
Lady Clarke
Thomas Forster
(born 1676/77)
Graphite on vellum, 1695
11 x 8.3cm

Page numbers in *italics* are for illustrations; titles in *italics* are for paintings unless otherwise indicated

Asselyn, Jan *34*, 35

Backer, Jacob 33, *33*
Banks, Lettice Mary 70, *70*
Barker, Thomas 8, 10, 78, *78*, 79
Beckford, William 6
Birth of Venus, The (cameo) 6, *7*
Blaker, Hugh 10
Blomfield, Reginald 12
Bogle, John *62*
Bow Porcelain Factory 51, *51*
British paintings
  'fancy' and literary 82–5
  landscapes 86–7
  portraits 56–61, 65, 70–9, 82–3
  portrait miniatures 62–3, 65
bronzes 18–19
Brueghel, Pieter, the Younger 28–9, *28*, *29*
Byam Family, The 72, 73

Carter Thelwall, Revd Robert, and his Family 61, *61*
Charlotte Augusta, Princess of Wales 63, *63*

Chelsea Porcelain Factory *43*, *50*, 51
Chinese porcelain 46, *47*
Clarges, Lady Louisa (Louisa Skrine) 75, *75*
Clarke, Alicia and Jane 60, 61
Clarke, Lady Dorothy 63, 88
Clive, Kitty (Bow porcelain) 51
Constable, John 86, 87
Cussans, Catherine 6, 9

Daniel, Abraham *62*, 63
Dead Soldier, The 84
Deserter Pardon'd, The 84, *85*
Devis, Arthur *60*, 61
Diana and Actaeon (maiolica) *16*
Diana and Endymion (sculpture) 68, *68–9*
Dottin, Abel Rous 76, *76*
Dottin, Samuel 76, *76*
Dutch paintings 7–8, 26, 28–35

Eissler, Johan *24*, 25
embroideries 22–3
English porcelain 42–3, 50–3, 66
Entombment, The 38, 39

fan leaf 64, *64–5*
Fanelli, Francesco *18*, 19
Flatford Mill from the Bridge 86, 87

Forster, Thomas 63, *88*

Gainsborough, Thomas 70, 72–5
German school 26, *26*
Giles, James *50*
glassware 45, *45*
Gouyn, Charles *66*
Guardi, Francesco 37, *37*

Hamlet, William *6*
Hennell, David *44*
Hill, John 11, *11*
Hillebrandt, Friedrich 20
Hoare, William 70, *70*, *71*
Holburne, Admiral Francis 5
Holburne, Captain Francis 5–6, *6*
Holburne, Mary Anne Barbara 8, *8*, 9, 11
Holburne, Sir Thomas William 4, 5, 6–8, *8*
Holburne Museum 8–10, *9*, 12–13, *12*, *13*
Hone, Nathaniel 64, *65*
Hoskins, John (circle of) *62*, 63
Hyde, Laurence, Earl of Rochester 56–7, *56*

Italian paintings 36–9

Jacob's Ladder (raised work) 23, *23*
Jagger, Charles *4*, 5
Japanese porcelain 46, *46*
Johnson, J. *21*
Jones, Charlotte *62*, 63
Jones, Priscilla 78, 79
Judgement of Paris, The 26, *26*

Kandler, Charles Frederick 40, 41
Kauffmann, Angelica 76, *77*

Lady's Maid Soaping Linen 83, *83*
landscape paintings 34–7, 86–7
Lawrence, Thomas 76, *76*, 77
Loggon, Thomas 64, *64–5*
Love Songs and Matches 82, *82*
Lutkin, William *44*, 45

maiolica 16–17
Mask of Truth, The 39, *39*
Maugham Collection 80–1
Meissen porcelain 48, *48*, *49*
miniatures, portrait 62–3, 65
Morland, George 84, *85*
Morland, Henry Robert 82, *83*

Nash, Richard ('Beau') 64, *65*
Nattes, Jean-Claude 11
Northern European paintings 26–35
Nugent, Robert Craggs 74, 75

Orme, Garton at the Spinet 57, *57*

paintings 7–8, 10
  see also British paintings; Dutch paintings; Italian paintings;

Maugham Collection; Northern European paintings
Panini, Giovanni Paolo *36*, 37
Parry, Eric 13
patchboxes *67*
Pembroke Castle *86*, 87
Pickenoy, Nicolaes *32*, 33
Pitt Family of Encombe 70, *71*
Plura, Giuseppe 68, *68–9*
portraits 56–61, 65, 70–9, 82–3
  miniatures 62–3, 65
Priest, William *43*
Pulteney, Henrietta Laura 76, *77*

Ramsay, Allan *58*, 59, *59*
Restoration of Charles II (raised work) 22–3, *22*
Richardson, Jonathan, the Elder 57, *57*
Robbing the Bird's Nest 28–9, *28*
Robertson, William 41, *41*
Rocca, Michele 39, *39*
Roch, Sampson Towgood *62*, 63
Rochard, Simon Jacques 63, *63*
Romanelli, Giovanni Francesco *38*, 39
Rosenberg, Charles 65, *65*
Russell, John 82, *82*

Sargent, John, the Elder *58*, 59
Sargent, Rosamund, née Chambers 59, *59*
Schuppe, John *43*
sculpture 18–19, 68–9
Sèvres Porcelain Factory 48, *48*
Shaw, William II *43*
silverware 20–1, 24–5, 40–1, *43*
spoons, early silver 20–1
St George and the Dragon (bronze statuette) *18*, 19
Stephany and Dresch 6, *7*
Stubbs, George 61, *61*
Susini, Antonio 19, *19*
Sydney Hotel and Gardens 11–12, *11*, *12*

Temptation of St Anthony, The 30, *30*
toyshops, Georgian Bath *67*
Trafalgar, Battle of 5
Turner, J.M.W. *86*, 87

Udney, Mrs Martha *62*

Venne, Jan van der 30, *30*
Visit of the Godfather, The 29, *29*

Wedgwood Ceramic Factory 52–3
Wissing, Willem 56–7, *56*
Witcombe Cabinet 54–5
Worcester Porcelain Factory 42, *43*, *50*, 51
Wouverman, Philips 35, *35*
Wright, Joseph, of Derby 84, *84*

Zoffany, Johan *81*